Jerusalem fell to the Babylonians after a
bloody battle, and thousands of Jews were
deported. Their anguished exile from their
homeland lasted seventy years.
But Cyrus the Great granted them freedom
once again, and on their return home, they
began to rebuild their great city and their
wonderful Temple devoted to the continuing
worship of God.

Here is the fourth in the unique series that
brings all of the excitement, drama and
color of the Bible in words and pictures
from the world's greatest, truest Book!

The Picture Bible for All Ages

VOLUME 4

THE CAPTIVITY

1 KINGS 21:9—MALACHI

Script by Iva Hoth

Illustrations by Andre Le Blanc

Bible Editor, C. Elvan Olmstead, Ph.D.

David C. Cook Publishing Co.
850 NORTH GROVE AVENUE • ELGIN, IL 60120
In Canada: David C. Cook Publishing (Canada) Ltd., Weston, Ontario M9L 1T4

THE CAPTIVITY
First printing, June 1973
Second printing, September 1973
Third printing, October 1973
Fourth printing, January 1974
Fifth printing, February 1974

© 1973 David C. Cook Publishing Co., Elgin, IL 60120
All Rights Reserved. This book, or parts thereof,
may not be reproduced in any form without permission
of the publisher, except by a reviewer who wishes
to quote brief passages in connection with a review
in a magazine or newspaper.
Published by David C. Cook Publishing Co.
Printed in United States of America by Offset Paperbacks.
Library of Congress Catalog Card Number: 73-78171
ISBN: 0-912692-16-2

ILLUSTRATED STORIES

THE CAPTIVITY

Behold, the days come,
that all that is in thine house,
and that which thy fathers
have laid up in store . . .
shall be carried to Babylon.

ISAIAH 39: 6

The Price of a Vineyard

FROM I KINGS 21: 9—22: 29

QUEEN JEZEBEL SIGNED KING AHAB'S NAME TO LETTERS SHE SENT TO THE ELDERS AND NOBLES OF THE CITY. WHEN THE MEN RECEIVE THE MESSAGES...

THIS SAYS WE ARE TO ACCUSE NABOTH OF CURSING GOD AND THE KING--AND TO HAVE HIM STONED TO DEATH.

NABOTH? HE'S A GOOD MAN. THIS LOOKS LIKE THE WORK OF JEZEBEL.

RIGHT--THE MESSENGER SAID THE LETTER CAME FROM THE QUEEN HERSELF.

DO WE DARE DISOBEY THESE ORDERS? THEY CAME FROM THE QUEEN!

NOT IF WE VALUE OUR LIVES. NO MAN CAN SAVE NABOTH IF JEZEBEL WANTS HIS LIFE.

10

11

AHAB IS SO FRIGHTENED BY ELIJAH'S PROPHECY THAT FOR A TIME HE SEEKS GOD'S FAVOR. BUT WHEN THE KING OF JUDAH COMES TO VISIT HIM, HE PREPARES FOR WAR IN SPITE OF GOD'S WARNING.

THE SYRIANS TOOK ONE OF MY CITIES. WILL YOU HELP ME DRIVE THEM OUT?

YOUR WAR IS MY WAR, AHAB.

THE ARMIES ARE FORMED, AND THE TWO KINGS LEAD THEIR FORCES ACROSS THE JORDAN RIVER TOWARD THE CONQUERED CITY. BUT AT THE THOUGHT OF THE COMING BATTLE, AHAB BECOMES FRIGHTENED.

I'LL DISGUISE MYSELF SO THE ENEMY WON'T RECOGNIZE ME!

14

SO THEY SET OUT TOGETHER. GOD HAS REVEALED TO BOTH OF THEM THAT THIS IS ELIJAH'S LAST JOURNEY, BUT THEY SAY NOTHING. WHEN THEY REACH THE JORDAN RIVER, ELIJAH STRIKES IT WITH HIS CLOAK-- THE WATERS PART, AND THEY WALK ACROSS ON DRY LAND.

ON THE OTHER SIDE, ELIJAH STOPS--AS IF HE HAS REACHED THE END OF HIS JOURNEY.

IS THERE ANY REQUEST YOU WANT TO MAKE BEFORE GOD TAKES ME AWAY?

YES, GIVE ME THE SPIRITUAL POWER TO CARRY ON THE WORK YOU HAVE BEEN DOING FOR GOD.

ONLY GOD CAN GRANT YOUR WISH. YOU'LL HAVE TO WAIT AND SEE WHAT HAPPENS...

15

OUR BIBLE IN PICTURES
Chariot of Fire
FROM II KINGS 2: 11-18; 4: 1

ELISHA ASKS FOR THE SPIRITUAL POWER TO CARRY ON ELIJAH'S WORK. AND ELIJAH PROMISES: "IF YOU SEE ME WHEN I AM TAKEN FROM YOU, IT WILL BE A SIGN THAT GOD HAS GRANTED YOUR WISH." SUDDENLY A CHARIOT OF FIRE SWEEPS DOWN AND SEPARATES ELIJAH FROM ELISHA, AND ELIJAH IS TAKEN UP IN A WHIRLWIND...

ELIJAH! ELIJAH! I SEE NOW--THE POWER THAT PROTECTED AND GUIDED YOU IS GREATER THAN ALL THE ARMIES OF EARTH!

FOR A LONG TIME ELISHA STANDS LOOKING UP INTO THE SKY. THEN, PICKING UP THE PROPHET'S CLOAK, HE TURNS BACK. AT THE JORDAN HE STRIKES THE WATER WITH HIS CLOAK--AND THE WATERS PART.

O GOD, I THANK THEE FOR THE GIFT OF THY POWER.

16

17

UNDER THE QUEEN'S INFLUENCE MEN FEEL FREE TO TAKE ADVANTAGE OF THOSE WHO HAVE OPPOSED THE QUEEN.

YOUR HUSBAND OWED ME MONEY WHEN HE WAS ALIVE. PAY ME WHAT HE OWED, OR I'LL TAKE YOUR SONS AS SLAVES!

SLAVES! NO! O GOD, WHAT CAN I DO?

THERE'S ONLY ONE THING YOU CAN DO. HAVE THE BOYS READY TOMORROW. REMEMBER, THE LAW IS ON MY SIDE.

IN DESPERATION THE WOMAN SEARCHES FOR ELISHA.

HELP ME! HELP ME!

WHAT IS THE MATTER?

MY SONS! THE MONEYLENDER WILL TAKE THEM AS SLAVES-- TOMORROW-- UNLESS I GIVE HIM THE MONEY MY HUSBAND OWED HIM. AND I HAVE NO MONEY NOW.

DON'T WORRY-- I PROMISE THAT YOU WILL HAVE A SURPRISE FOR THE MONEYLENDER WHEN HE COMES...

18

OUR BIBLE IN PICTURES
A Miracle of Oil
FROM II KINGS 4: 2-7

ELISHA PROMISES A SURPRISE FOR THE MONEYLENDER WHO DEMANDS THAT A WIDOW GIVE HER SONS IN PAYMENT FOR A DEBT SHE CANNOT PAY.

TELL ME WHAT YOU HAVE IN YOUR HOUSE.

ONLY A JAR OF OIL.

BORROW ALL THE EMPTY JARS YOU CAN FROM THE NEIGHBORS. POUR THE OIL INTO THE JARS, AND TRUST GOD TO HELP YOU.

THE WOMAN QUICKLY BEGINS TO COLLECT ALL THE JARS SHE CAN.

MORE JARS, MOTHER. BUT SURELY YOUR JAR IS EMPTY NOW.

NO. I HAVE FILLED THESE JARS, BUT THERE IS STILL MORE OIL. ELISHA SAID TO FILL ALL THE JARS WE COULD FIND.

19

THERE, THAT'S THE LAST JAR WE HAVE -- AND MINE IS STILL FULL. IT'S A MIRACLE.

SHE HURRIES WITH HER NEWS TO ELISHA...

EVERY JAR IS FILLED -- AND WITH THE VERY BEST OIL, TOO. HOW CAN I THANK YOU?

THANK GOD -- FOR IT WAS HE WHO HELPED YOU. NOW, SELL THE OIL, PAY THE MONEYLENDER, AND LIVE ON THE REST OF THE MONEY.

WITH A GRATEFUL HEART, THE WOMAN THANKS GOD FOR SAVING HER SONS. THEN SHE SELLS THE OIL, AND WAITS FOR THE MONEYLENDER. THE NEXT MORNING, EARLY...

WHERE ARE MY SLAVES? I TOLD YOU TO BE READY FOR ME.

I AM READY FOR YOU. COME OUT, BOYS.

A Prophet's Prescription

FROM II KINGS 5: 1-14a

AN ISRAELITE GIRL, KIDNAPPED BY SYRIAN RAIDERS, BECOMES A SERVANT TO THE WIFE OF SYRIA'S GENERAL, NAAMAN.

THANK YOU, DEAR, I'M NOT HUNGRY.

ARE YOU ILL?

NO, BUT MY HUSBAND IS. HE HAS LEPROSY AND NO ONE CAN CURE HIM.

I KNOW A PROPHET OF GOD IN ISRAEL WHO CAN.

NAAMAN'S WIFE BELIEVES THE GIRL AND RUNS TO TELL HER HUSBAND. NAAMAN QUICKLY TAKES THE NEWS TO THE KING.

I CAN'T BELIEVE IT, NAAMAN, BUT I'LL GIVE YOU A LETTER TO TAKE TO THE KING OF ISRAEL.

IN SAMARIA, THE CAPITAL OF ISRAEL, NAAMAN HAS THE LETTER DELIVERED TO KING JEHORAM. THE LETTER DOES NOT MENTION ELISHA, SO THE KING MISINTERPRETS IT.

WHAT'S THIS — THE KING OF SYRIA ASKS **ME** TO CURE HIS GENERAL?

AM I A GOD THAT I CAN CURE AN INCURABLE DISEASE? IS THE KING OF SAMARIA TRYING TO PICK A QUARREL WITH ME?

REPORTS OF KING JEHORAM'S PROBLEM SPREAD THROUGHOUT THE CITY. WHEN ELISHA HEARS THEM HE SENDS HIS SERVANT TO THE KING.

ELISHA SAYS IF YOU SEND NAAMAN TO HIM, THE GENERAL WILL LEARN THE POWER OF GOD'S PROPHET.

I'LL SEND WORD TO NAAMAN AT ONCE.

NAAMAN LOSES NO TIME IN GOING TO ELISHA'S HOUSE WHERE HE IS MET BY A SERVANT.

GREETINGS, NAAMAN. ELISHA SAYS THAT IF YOU WILL WASH SEVEN TIMES IN THE JORDAN RIVER YOU WILL BE CURED.

WASH IN THE JORDAN? THAT'S SILLY! I THOUGHT ELISHA WOULD CALL ON HIS GOD TO CURE ME.

NAAMAN THINKS HE HAS BEEN MADE A FOOL OF— AND IN A RAGE HE DRIVES AWAY.

THINK AGAIN, NAAMAN. IF ELISHA HAD ASKED YOU TO DO SOMETHING HARD, YOU WOULD HAVE DONE IT. WHY NOT DO THIS EASY THING HE ASKS?

THE GENERAL TAKES HIS SERVANT'S ADVICE AND GOES TO THE JORDAN RIVER.

I DON'T SEE HOW THIS MUDDY WATER WILL CURE LEPROSY.

24

Surrounded

FROM II KINGS 5: 14-16; 6: 8-16

THEN NAAMAN RETURNS TO HIS HOME IN SYRIA.

I THANK GOD EVERY DAY FOR HEALING ME, AND I OWE IT ALL TO ELISHA...

AND TO THE LITTLE GIRL WHO ALSO BELIEVES IN ELISHA'S GOD.

BUT THE HEALING OF NAAMAN DOES NOT KEEP THE KING OF SYRIA FROM PLOTTING AGAINST ISRAEL.

MY SPIES TELL ME THAT THE KING OF ISRAEL WILL SOON BE RETURNING TO SAMARIA. SET UP AN AMBUSH AND CAPTURE HIM.

A FEW DAYS LATER ON THE ROAD TO SAMARIA...

STOP! ELISHA SENDS WORD FOR YOU TO TAKE ANOTHER ROAD. THE SYRIANS ARE WAITING ON THIS ROAD TO CAPTURE YOU.

FOR DAYS THE SYRIAN SOLDIERS WAIT FOR THE ISRAELITE KING -- BUT HE DOESN'T COME. AGAIN THE SYRIAN KING SETS A TRAP AND AGAIN ELISHA WARNS HIS KING TO ESCAPE. FINALLY THE SYRIAN KING BECOMES SO ANGRY THAT HE ACCUSES HIS OWN MEN OF TREASON.

WE'RE NOT GUILTY, O KING. IT'S ELISHA, THE PROPHET IN ISRAEL, WHO IS TELLING YOUR PLANS.

ELISHA, IS IT? HAVE OUR SPIES FIND OUT WHERE HE IS AND I'LL SEND AN ARMY TO GET HIM.

A FEW DAYS LATER...

I HAVE GOOD NEWS FOR YOU -- ELISHA IS AT DOTHAN.

SEND AN ARMY AT ONCE TO SURROUND THE CITY.

THE SYRIANS MARCH -- AND SET UP THEIR CAMP BY NIGHT. THE NEXT MORNING -- ELISHA'S SERVANT RISES EARLY AND SEES THE SYRIAN ARMY

ELISHA! WE'RE SURROUNDED -- BY THE WHOLE SYRIAN ARMY!

FEAR NOT -- THERE'S MORE POWER ON OUR SIDE THAN ON THEIRS.

One Against an Army

FROM II KINGS 6: 17-24

THE ARMY OF HEAVEN IS WITH ELISHA!

ELISHA'S SERVANT IS FRIGHTENED WHEN HE SEES THE SYRIAN ARMY. BUT AS ELISHA PRAYS, THE SERVANT LOOKS UP TO SEE CHARIOTS OF FIRE SURROUNDING THE PROPHET.

TO SAVE THE CITY FROM ATTACK, ELISHA AND HIS SERVANT GO OUT TO MEET THE ENEMY. AT ONCE THE SYRIAN SOLDIERS CLOSE IN ON THEM. BUT ELISHA PRAYS, AND SUDDENLY...

I CAN'T SEE--WHAT'S HAPPENED?

I'M BLIND-- I--

COME WITH ME. I KNOW THE ONE YOU SEEK, AND I'LL TAKE YOU TO HIM.

TO THE AMAZEMENT OF THE SYRIANS, THEY ARE GIVEN FOOD AND TOLD TO RETURN HOME.

I CAN'T BELIEVE IT! WE TRIED TO KILL BOTH THE KING AND ELISHA-- AND NOW THEY TREAT US LIKE FRIENDS!

BACK HOME, THE SYRIANS TELL ABOUT THE KINDNESS OF THE ISRAELITES, AND FOR A TIME THERE IS PEACE BETWEEN THE TWO NATIONS. BUT AFTER A WHILE...

WE'LL CUT OFF ALL FOOD SUPPLIES TO SAMARIA, SURROUND IT, AND STARVE THE PEOPLE INTO SURRENDER.

EXCELLENT! AND THE LONGER THEY HOLD OUT, THE EASIER THEY WILL BE TO TAKE.

SO THE SYRIAN ARMY PITCHES ITS TENTS AROUND THE WALLS OF SAMARIA AND WAITS...

I WONDER HOW LONG THEY CAN HOLD OUT.

A Starving City

FROM II KINGS 6: 25—7: 5

SAMARIA, THE CAPITAL OF ISRAEL, IS SURROUNDED BY THE SYRIAN ARMY. THE CITY MAKES A BRAVE STAND TO HOLD OUT, BUT AS MONTHS PASS, AND NO FOOD IS ALLOWED INTO THE GATES, THE PEOPLE PLEAD FOR ACTION FROM THE KING.

OUR CHILDREN ARE DYING. WE MUST HAVE FOOD.

I'D RATHER TAKE MY CHANCES FIGHTING THE ENEMY THAN STARVING TO DEATH!

WHO HAS STRENGTH ENOUGH TO FIGHT NOW?

THE ANXIOUS KING IS WILLING TO WAIT UNTIL THE NEXT DAY, BUT OUTSIDE THE CITY FOUR LEPERS HAVE NOT HEARD ELISHA'S PROPHECY...

I'M STARVING. I'M GOING TO TRY TO BREAK INTO THE CITY AND GET SOME FOOD.

WHY DO THAT? THERE'S NO FOOD IN THERE.

THEN LET'S GO OVER TO THE SYRIAN CAMP. MAYBE THEY'LL GIVE US SOMETHING TO EAT. MAYBE THEY'LL KILL US. EITHER WAY, THERE'S NOTHING TO LOSE-- WE'LL STARVE IF WE STAY HERE.

IN DESPERATION THE FOUR HUNGRY LEPERS APPROACH THE SYRIAN CAMP.

SOMETHING STRANGE IS GOING ON. THERE'S NOT A GUARD IN SIGHT. MAYBE IT'S A TRAP--

MAYBE IT IS-- BUT I'D RATHER DIE QUICKLY THAN STARVE TO DEATH. COME ON--

THERE'S NOBODY HERE!

33

The Missing Enemy

FROM II KINGS 7: 6-15

DRIVEN BY HUNGER, FOUR LEPERS FROM OUTSIDE THE WALLS OF SAMARIA GO TO THE ENEMY CAMP FOR FOOD. TO THEIR AMAZEMENT, THEY FIND IT DESERTED...

FOOD! ENOUGH FOR ALL OF US!

THIS STEW IS STILL WARM— THEY MUST HAVE JUST LEFT.

AND IN SUCH A HURRY THEY EVEN FORGOT THEIR GOLD.

THEIR HUNGER SATISFIED, THE LEPERS QUICKLY SEARCH THE SYRIAN TENTS.

MORE GOLD-- WE'RE RICH!

LOOK! WON'T PEOPLE BE SURPRISED TO SEE ME IN THIS?

SURPRISED? THEY'LL SAY YOU STOLE IT. THEN YOU'LL REALLY BE IN TROUBLE.

HE'S RIGHT-- LET'S HIDE EVERYTHING.

IT ISN'T RIGHT FOR US TO KEEP ALL OF THIS FOOD FROM THE STARVING PEOPLE IN THE CITY.

IF WE DON'T TELL THE GOOD NEWS, SOME PUNISHMENT MAY COME UPON US.

THE MEN GO BACK TO THE CITY AND POUND ON THE GATES UNTIL A GUARD ANSWERS.

THE SYRIANS ARE GONE!

GONE? WHERE? HOW DO YOU KNOW?

35

WE DON'T KNOW WHERE OR WHY--BUT WE WERE IN THEIR CAMP. THEY LEFT THEIR FOOD, TENTS, HORSES --EVERYTHING!

I'LL GET WORD TO THE KING RIGHT AWAY.

ROUSED FROM HIS BED, KING JEHORAM RECEIVES THE NEWS AND CALLS HIS ADVISERS.

IT'S A TRAP-- THE SYRIANS ARE WAITING IN AMBUSH TO CAPTURE US IF WE LEAVE THE CITY.

MAYBE -- BUT LET'S SEND OUT A FEW MEN TO SEE WHAT'S GOING ON.

THE KING'S MEN QUICKLY PICK UP THE SYRIAN TRAIL BY FOLLOWING THE CLOTHING, WEAPONS, AND VESSELS, DROPPED ALONG THE WAY.

WHAT COULD HAVE HAPPENED TO MAKE TRAINED SOLDIERS THROW AWAY THEIR WEAPONS AND RUN FOR THEIR LIVES?

LOOK-- MORE SHIELDS. THE SYRIANS ARE LETTING NOTHING SLOW THEM DOWN IN THEIR FLIGHT.

OUR BIBLE IN PICTURES

The Sound of Marching Men

FROM II KINGS 7: 14—9: 12

THE ISRAELITE SCOUTS FOLLOW THE FLEEING SYRIAN ARMY TO THE JORDAN RIVER. ALONG THE WAY THEY OVERTAKE ONE OF THE ENEMY SOLDIERS.

PULL UP--HERE'S ONE WHO DROPPED BEHIND. MAYBE HE CAN TELL US WHAT HAPPENED.

WHY DID YOU SYRIANS DESERT CAMP IN THE MIDDLE OF THE NIGHT?

WE WERE GOING TO BE ATTACKED! WE THOUGHT THE HITTITES WERE COMING FROM THE NORTH -- AND THE EGYPTIANS FROM THE SOUTH -- TO TRAP US.

38

IN SPITE OF THE FACT THAT GOD HAS SAVED ISRAEL, KING JEHORAM AND HIS MOTHER KEEP ON WORSHIPPING BAAL. WHEN ONE OF HIS BORDER CITIES IS ATTACKED BY THE KING OF SYRIA, JEHORAM GOES TO ITS DEFENSE. WOUNDED IN THE BATTLE, HE LEAVES CAPTAIN JEHU IN CHARGE AND RETURNS HOME.

WHILE THE KING IS AWAY FROM THE ARMY, ELISHA CALLS FOR A YOUNG PROPHET TO MAKE A QUICK JOURNEY FOR HIM.

TAKE THIS OIL -- GO OUT TO WHERE OUR ARMY IS CAMPED, AND DO WHAT I TELL YOU.

AT THE CAMP THE YOUNG PROPHET SEARCHES UNTIL HE FINDS A GROUP OF OFFICERS.

CAPTAIN JEHU! PLEASE COME WITH ME -- I MUST SPEAK TO YOU ALONE.

THUS SAYS THE LORD; "I HAVE ANOINTED YOU TO BE KING OVER ISRAEL, TO FIGHT FOR THOSE WHO WORSHIP ME, AND AGAINST THOSE WHO WORSHIP BAAL."

WHAT DID THAT FELLOW WANT?

HE WAS A MESSENGER FROM GOD -- AND HE ANOINTED ME KING -- KING OF ISRAEL!

WHAT'S GOING TO HAPPEN WHEN KING JEHORAM LEARNS OF THIS?

OUR BIBLE IN PICTURES

Revenge of Israel

FROM II KINGS 9: 13-32

JEHU, A CAPTAIN IN THE ARMY, HAS JUST BEEN ANOINTED KING OF ISRAEL. HIS MEN GO WILD WITH JOY! THEY BLOW THEIR TRUMPETS AND THROW DOWN THEIR GARMENTS TO MAKE A THRONE...

LONG LIVE THE KING!

JEHU IS KING!

MY FIRST JOB IS TO GET RID OF JEZEBEL'S SON, KING JEHORAM. ARE YOU WITH ME?

WE'RE WITH YOU -- TO A MAN.

JEHORAM IS IN JEZREEL. WE'LL HAVE TO GET TO HIM BEFORE HE LEARNS WHAT'S HAPPENED.

JEHU AND A COMPANY OF MEN SET OUT AT ONCE -- AND AS THEY APPROACH JEZREEL...

CHARIOTS! A WHOLE LINE OF THEM. THE LEADER MUST BE JEHU. HE'S DRIVING SO FAST.

WHEN THE NEWS REACHES KING JEHORAM, HE BELIEVES JEHU IS BRINGING NEWS OF THE WAR. SO, WITH HIS VISITOR, KING AHAZIAH OF JUDAH, HE RIDES OUT TO MEET JEHU.

DO YOU BRING NEWS OF PEACE?

HOW CAN THERE BE PEACE IN ISRAEL WHILE YOUR MOTHER, JEZEBEL, WORSHIPS BAAL?

TOO LATE, JEHORAM SEES THAT JEHU HAS COME TO OVERTHROW THE KINGDOM. HE TRIES TO ESCAPE, BUT JEHU'S ARROW STRIKES HIM DOWN.

THAT'S THE FIRST BLOW STRUCK FOR ISRAEL.

BUT NOT THE LAST! NOW JEZEBEL MUST PAY FOR HER SINS!

41

42

OUR BIBLE IN PICTURES
A Queen's Plot
FROM II KINGS 9: 32—11: 3

WHEN THE PALACE SERVANTS DISCOVER THAT JEHU IS NOW KING OF ISRAEL, THEY SHOW THEIR ALLEGIANCE TO HIM BY PUSHING QUEEN JEZEBEL FROM THE WINDOW TO HER DEATH IN THE STREET BELOW. SO JEZEBEL PAYS WITH HER LIFE FOR THE EVIL SHE HAS DONE -- AND ELIJAH'S PROPHECY IS FULFILLED. JEHU WIPES OUT THE WORSHIP OF BAAL IN ISRAEL.

DESTROY THE IDOL OF BAAL!

BREAK DOWN THE HEATHEN TEMPLE! FROM THIS DAY ON IT SHALL BE A PLACE TO DUMP REFUSE.

The Temple Secret
FROM II KINGS 11: 1-12

UNDER COVER OF DARKNESS THE TWO WOMEN HURRY TO THE TEMPLE OF GOD. THE HIGH PRIEST, JEHOIADA, ANSWERS THEIR FRANTIC KNOCK.

WE HAVE BABY JOASH. HELP US SAVE HIM FROM THE QUEEN.

COME IN-- HURRY!

ONLY THE PRIESTS USE THIS ROOM. JOASH WILL BE SAFE HERE AS LONG AS IT IS NECESSARY TO HIDE HIM.

46

A FEW HOURS LATER THE QUEEN'S OFFICER GIVES HIS REPORT.

THE KING'S RELATIVES HAVE BEEN PUT TO DEATH --AS YOU COMMANDED.

GOOD!

NOW THERE IS NO ONE TO SAY I CANNOT RULE JUDAH.

FOR SIX YEARS ATHALIAH RULES JUDAH WITH A CRUEL HAND UNTIL AT LAST THE PEOPLE BEGIN TO COMPLAIN. UNKNOWN TO THEM --IN A SECRET ROOM OF THE TEMPLE--YOUNG PRINCE JOASH IS BEING TRAINED BY THE HIGH PRIEST.

WHAT'S THIS?

THE IDOL BAAL--THE CAUSE OF ALL THE TROUBLE IN JUDAH. YOUR GRANDMOTHER WORSHIPS IT. WHEN YOU ARE KING, YOU MUST DESTROY IT AND LEAD YOUR PEOPLE BACK TO GOD.

NOW, TELL ME THE WORD OF GOD YOU HAVE LEARNED TODAY.

THOU SHALT LOVE THE LORD THY GOD WITH ALL THINE HEART, AND WITH ALL THY SOUL, AND WITH ALL THY MIGHT!

47

ONE DAY A PRIEST OF THE TEMPLE COMES TO JEHOIADA.

I PRAY THAT GOD WILL DELIVER JUDAH FROM THIS IDOL WORSHIP.

AND GOD HAS ANSWERED YOUR PRAYER. I HAVE SENT FOR ALL THE CAPTAINS OF THE GUARD TO MEET SECRETLY IN THE TEMPLE. COME--

IN THE TEMPLE...

MEN-- THIS IS PRINCE JOASH, YOUR RIGHTFUL RULER. I AM GOING TO CROWN HIM KING OF JUDAH ON THIS COMING SABBATH. BE THERE WITH ALL YOUR MEN TO PROTECT HIM.

THE NEXT SABBATH IN THE PALACE...

THE SOUND OF CHEERING --IT COMES FROM THE TEMPLE. I WONDER WHAT IT MEANS!

Boy King of Judah

FROM II KINGS 11: 13-21; II CHRONICLES 24: 1-23

50

UNDER THE GUIDANCE OF JEHOIADA, THE HIGH PRIEST, JOASH DESTROYS THE TEMPLE OF BAAL AND LEADS HIS PEOPLE BACK TO THE WORSHIP OF GOD. THE HOUSE OF GOD IS REPAIRED, AND FOR YEARS JUDAH PROSPERS. BUT WHEN JEHOIADA DIES, JOASH IS TOO WEAK TO STAND UP UNDER THE PRESSURE OF THOSE WHO WOULD TURN HIM AWAY FROM GOD. FINALLY, JEHOIADA'S SON, ZECHARIAH, GOES TO THE KING...

KING JOASH, I SPEAK TO YOU AS MY FATHER WOULD SPEAK. YOUR PEOPLE ARE RETURNING TO BAAL AND FORSAKING GOD. JUDAH WILL BE DESTROYED UNLESS YOU STOP THEM!

AS SOON AS ZECHARIAH LEAVES, THE WORSHIPERS OF BAAL GIVE **THEIR** ADVICE.

ZECHARIAH IS A TROUBLE-MAKER.

HE SHOULD BE PUT TO DEATH BEFORE HE TURNS ALL JUDAH AGAINST YOU.

YOU'RE RIGHT. STIR UP THE PEOPLE SO THAT THEY WILL GET RID OF HIM.

AND SO JOASH, WHO WAS ONCE A GOOD KING, LISTENS TO EVIL ADVICE. ZECHARIAH IS STONED TO DEATH BY A MOB--AND SOON HIS PROPHECY OF DISASTER COMES TRUE...

Dagger in the Night

FROM II KINGS 12—18: 10

WHEN KING JOASH TURNED AWAY FROM GOD, ZECHARIAH PREDICTED DISASTER. IT COMES SOON-- IN AN ATTACK BY THE KING OF SYRIA WHO IS ON A CAMPAIGN OF CONQUEST. DURING THE ATTACK THE MEN WHO HAD ADVISED JOASH AGAINST ZECHARIAH ARE KILLED. IN AN ATTEMPT TO SAVE JERUSALEM, JOASH TRIES TO BUY OFF THE ENEMY.

GIFTS FROM MY LORD, KING JOASH OF JUDAH. HE ASKS THAT YOU ACCEPT THEM AND LEAVE JERUSALEM IN PEACE.

TELL YOUR KING I ACCEPT HIS OFFER.

HAVING ACQUIRED AN EASY FORTUNE, THE KING OF SYRIA CALLS BACK HIS ARMY AND MARCHES ON. JERUSALEM IS SAVED, BUT JOASH FALLS GRAVELY ILL.

HOW IS THE KING TODAY?

NO BETTER-- NO WORSE. TOO BAD THE SYRIANS DIDN'T KILL THE KING ALONG WITH THE MEN WHO ADVISED HIM TO MURDER ZECHARIAH. WITH THEM GONE WE COULD SAVE JUDAH --IF IT WEREN'T...

IF YOU'RE THINKING WHAT I AM--

SH! THIS ISN'T THE TIME.

BUT THAT NIGHT-- WHEN ALL THE PALACE IS ASLEEP...

REMEMBER-- WE'RE DOING THIS TO SAVE OUR COUNTRY.

SO KING JOASH IS MURDERED-- BY HIS OWN MEN. FOR ALMOST A HUNDRED YEARS JUDAH IS RULED BY KINGS WHO WAVER BETWEEN WORSHIPING GOD AND HEATHEN IDOLS. THEN HEZEKIAH COMES TO THE THRONE...

53

54

Test of a City

FROM II CHRONICLES 32: 1-20

THE KING OF ASSYRIA CONQUERS THE TEN TRIBES OF ISRAEL, BUT SEVERAL YEARS PASS BEFORE THE ASSYRIANS MAKE AN ATTACK AGAINST JUDAH. NOW WORD COMES TO KING HEZEKIAH THAT THE ASSYRIAN ARMY IS LAYING SIEGE TO SOME OF THE WALLED CITIES OF JUDAH.

HIS NEXT MOVE WILL BE AGAINST JERUSALEM. WE MUST PREPARE TO DEFEND THE CITY.

AT HEZEKIAH'S DIRECTION, WORKERS BUILD A TUNNEL BETWEEN A SPRING OUTSIDE THE WALLS TO A POOL WITHIN THE CITY.

THIS WILL DIRECT THE FLOW OF WATER TO US AND CUT OFF THE WATER SUPPLY FOR THE ASSYRIANS.

MY BROTHERS ARE HELPING TO BUILD UP THE WALLS. THANK GOD WE HAVE A RULER WHO WILL DEFEND US.

THEN HEZEKIAH CALLS THE PEOPLE TOGETHER...

DO NOT BE AFRAID. THERE IS MORE POWER ON OUR SIDE THAN ON THE SIDE OF THE ENEMY. THE LORD GOD IS WITH US.

BUT INSTEAD OF MAKING AN ARMED ATTACK ON THE CITY, THE ASSYRIAN KING SENDS A TASK FORCE TO TRY TO FRIGHTEN THE PEOPLE OF JERUSALEM INTO SURRENDERING.

WE HAVE CONQUERED OTHER CITIES AND COUNTRIES. WHAT MAKES YOU THINK YOUR GOD CAN SAVE YOU?

AFTER A WHILE THIS KIND OF ATTACK BEGINS TO HAVE ITS EFFECT.

HOW DO WE KNOW GOD WILL SAVE US?

OTHER CITIES HAVE FALLEN. AND, REMEMBER, IT WAS THE ASSYRIANS WHO TOOK ISRAEL.

57

A Foolish King

FROM II CHRONICLES 32: 21—33: 12

WHEN THE ASSYRIANS SUDDENLY STOP THREATENING THE PEOPLE OF JERUSALEM, KING HEZEKIAH SENDS MEN TO SCOUT THE ENEMY CAMP. THEY FIND IT STRANGELY QUIET.

WHY-- THEY'RE ASLEEP, OR--

A PLAGUE MUST HAVE STRUCK DOWN THE MAIN FORCE OF THE ENEMY.

AT THE NEWS, ALL JERUSALEM GOES WILD WITH JOY...

HEZEKIAH SAID GOD WAS ON OUR SIDE.

AND GOD DOESN'T FORSAKE THOSE WHO BELIEVE AND TRUST HIM ...

NEVER AGAIN WHILE HEZEKIAH LIVES DO THE ASSYRIANS TRY TO TAKE JERUSALEM. HEZEKIAH CONTINUES TO LEAD HIS PEOPLE IN THEIR WORSHIP OF GOD, AND THEY ARE HAPPY. AT HIS DEATH, HIS YOUNG SON, MANASSEH, IS CROWNED KING.

NO SOONER IS MANASSEH ON THE THRONE THAN THE FOLLOWERS OF BAAL BEGIN THEIR CAMPAIGN TO LEAD HIM AWAY FROM GOD.

TO BECOME RICH AND POWERFUL AS THE ASSYRIANS, WE SHOULD WORSHIP IDOLS, AS THEY DO.

MANASSEH LISTENS TO THEIR ADVICE, AND RESTORES IDOL WORSHIP IN ISRAEL. HE EVEN DARES TO PLACE AN IDOL IN THE TEMPLE OF GOD.

BUT WORSHIPING THE IDOLS OF THE SURROUNDING NATIONS DOES NOT SAVE MANASSEH. THE ASSYRIAN KING SUSPECTS MANASSEH IS PLOTTING AGAINST HIM AND SENDS TROOPS TO JERUSALEM. IN A SURPRISE MOVE THE ASSYRIANS OVERCOME MANASSEH'S FORCES AND TAKE THE KING PRISONER.

60

OUR BIBLE IN PICTURES
The Lost Book
FROM II CHRONICLES 33: 13—34: 18; II KINGS 22: 1-10

IN AN ASSYRIAN DUNGEON, KING MANASSEH OF JUDAH REPENTS FOR DISOBEYING GOD, AND ASKS FORGIVENESS. ONE DAY HE IS SUDDENLY BROUGHT BEFORE THE KING OF ASSYRIA.

REMOVE HIS CHAINS. TAKE HIM HOME AND LET HIM RULE JUDAH AGAIN-- UNDER MY COMMAND.

NO ONE KNOWS WHAT PROMPTED THE ASSYRIAN KING TO FREE MANASSEH --BUT WHEN HE RETURNS TO JERUSALEM HIS PEOPLE WELCOME HIM...

THE KING HAS RETURNED!

LONG LIVE THE KING OF JUDAH!

BUT THE PEOPLE ARE AMAZED AT HIS FIRST SPEECH...

I WAS WRONG TO TURN AWAY FROM GOD. DESTROY THE IDOLS, AND JOIN ME IN WORSHIPING GOD.

MANASSEH TRIES TO SAVE HIS NATION, BUT IT IS TOO LATE. MOST OF THE PEOPLE CONTINUE TO WORSHIP IDOLS. MANASSEH DIES, AND AFTER TWO YEARS, HIS EIGHT-YEAR-OLD GRANDSON, JOSIAH, COMES TO THE THRONE.

AS THE KING GROWS UP, THE IDOL WORSHIPERS TRY TO INFLUENCE JOSIAH, BUT THE YOUNG KING REMAINS TRUE TO GOD. HE RULES JUDAH WITH A FIRM BUT JUST HAND. ONE DAY HE CALLS FOR THREE OF HIS OFFICIALS.

THE WALLS OF THE TEMPLE ARE CRUMBLING-- I WANT THEM REPAIRED IMMEDIATELY.

63

A Prophetess Speaks

FROM II KINGS 22: 11—24: 20; II CHRONICLES 34: 19—36: 16

THE SCRIBE READS TO KING JOSIAH FROM THE LOST BOOK THAT HAS BEEN FOUND IN THE TEMPLE WALLS.

GOD'S LAWS ARE CLEARLY STATED -- AND SO IS THE PUNISHMENT FOR ANYONE WHO DISOBEYS THEM.

THEN JUDAH IS DOOMED! FOR IT HAS BROKEN GOD'S LAW MANY TIMES.

JOSIAH IS SO UPSET THAT HE QUICKLY SENDS SEVERAL HIGH-RANKING OFFICIALS TO THE PROPHETESS HULDAH.

THE KING HAS SENT US TO ASK FOR A MESSAGE FROM GOD ABOUT THE BOOK WE HAVE JUST READ.

THUS SAITH THE LORD: BECAUSE JUDAH HAS DISOBEYED ME, JUDAH SHALL BE DESTROYED... BUT THE DESTRUCTION WILL NOT COME IN THE DAYS OF JOSIAH.

HOPING HE MAY YET WIN GOD'S FORGIVENESS FOR HIS NATION, JOSIAH CALLS A MEETING OF THE PEOPLE.

I HAVE READ GOD'S LAWS TO YOU. LET US NOW PROMISE TO OBEY THEM FROM THIS DAY ON. AND MAY GOD HAVE MERCY ON US.

AT JOSIAH'S COMMAND PAGAN WORSHIP IS WIPED OUT IN ALL THE LAND. OBJECTS USED IN IDOL WORSHIP ARE REMOVED FROM GOD'S TEMPLE IN JERUSALEM, TAKEN OUTSIDE THE CITY, AND BURNED.

THEN JOSIAH CALLS THE PEOPLE TO KEEP THE FEAST OF THE PASSOVER.

THIS REMINDS US OF HOW GOD DELIVERED OUR FORE-FATHERS FROM SLAVERY IN EGYPT CENTURIES AGO.

WHILE JOSIAH LIVES, JUDAH OBEYS THE LAWS OF GOD. BUT AFTER HIS DEATH, ONE KING AFTER ANOTHER TURNS BACK TO THE WORSHIP OF IDOLS. LACKING GOD'S HELP, JUDAH COMES UNDER THE CONTROL OF A NEW WORLD POWER, BABYLONIA.

JUDAH IS ALLOWED TO REMAIN UNDER ITS OWN RULERS, BUT AFTER KING ZEDEKIAH COMES TO THE THRONE HE FOOLISHLY TRIES TO REGAIN HIS COUNTRY'S INDEPENDENCE. IN REPLY THE GREAT BABYLONIAN ARMY SETS OUT...

The Fall of Jerusalem

FROM II CHRONICLES 36: 17-20; II KINGS 25: 1-11

FOR TWO YEARS AND A HALF, FORCES FROM THE GREAT BABYLONIAN ARMY BESIEGE THE CITY OF JERUSALEM. AT LAST THEY BREAK THROUGH THE WALL ...

THAT NIGHT KING ZEDEKIAH AND HIS ARMY TRY TO ESCAPE.

IF WE CAN MAKE IT TO THE HILL REGION EAST OF THE JORDAN, THEY'LL NEVER FIND US.

IT'S OUR ONLY CHANCE --IF THEY CAPTURE US...

BUT THE BABYLONIANS PURSUE THEM, AND ZEDEKIAH IS CAPTURED BEFORE HE CAN REACH THE RIVER. HE IS BLINDED AND TAKEN TO BABYLON.

HUNGRY, WEARY, AND AFRAID, THE PEOPLE OF JERUSALEM ARE FORCED TO BEGIN THE LONG MARCH OF 900 MILES FROM JERUSALEM TO BABYLON--AS CAPTIVES.

GOD HAS FORSAKEN US.

NO. GOD WARNED US, BUT WE WOULD NOT LISTEN. IT IS WE WHO HAVE FORSAKEN GOD!

68

69

Return of the Captives

FROM EZRA 1, 2

FROM THE MOMENT THEY ARE CARRIED AWAY AS CAPTIVES TO BABYLON, THE JEWS DREAM OF RETURNING TO THEIR HOMELAND, JUDAH. THE BOOK OF **EZRA** TELLS WHAT HAPPENS TO THAT DREAM.

FOR MANY YEARS THE JEWS LIVE AS CAPTIVES OF THE GREAT BABYLONIAN EMPIRE. THEY WATCH ANXIOUSLY AS PERSIA, A STRONG COUNTRY TO THE EAST, RISES UP TO CHALLENGE BABYLON.

WHEN THE PERSIAN ARMY APPEARS OUTSIDE THE CITY WALLS, KING BELSHAZZAR IS SO SURE OF BABYLON'S STRENGTH THAT HE SPENDS THE NIGHT IN A DRUNKEN FEAST WITH HIS COURT. PERSIAN TROOPS STEAL INTO THE CITY-- INVADE THE PALACE--AND SLAY BELSHAZZAR. WITHIN HOURS THE BABYLONIAN EMPIRE FALLS TO PERSIA.

TWO WEEKS LATER KING CYRUS OF PERSIA RIDES TRIUMPHANTLY INTO THE CITY.

SO THAT'S OUR NEW RULER. I WONDER-- DOES THIS MEAN GOOD OR EVIL FOR US JEWS?

I'VE HEARD THAT CYRUS IS A JUST MAN. WE'LL HAVE TO WAIT AND SEE.

SOON AFTER CYRUS TAKES OVER THE BABYLONIAN EMPIRE, AN OFFICIAL ANNOUNCEMENT IS READ.

THESE ARE THE WORDS OF KING CYRUS: THE GOD OF ISRAEL COMMANDS THAT A HOUSE BE BUILT FOR HIM IN JERUSALEM. ANY OF HIS PEOPLE WHO WANT TO DO SO MAY RETURN. THOSE WHO DO NOT GO BACK SHOULD GIVE OF THEIR POSSESSIONS TO HELP THOSE WHO RETURN TO JUDAH.

GIFTS OF MONEY, HORSES, MULES, CAMELS, GOLD AND SILVER, FOOD AND CLOTHING POUR IN. AT LAST THE DAY COMES WHEN THE GREAT CARAVAN IS READY TO LEAVE.

THANK GOD, I'LL SEE MY HOMELAND AGAIN.

A City Rises Again

FROM EZRA 3—10

ALTHOUGH THE CITY OF JERUSALEM IS IN RUINS, THE JEWS WHO HAVE RETURNED FROM CAPTIVITY IN BABYLON SET TO WORK TO REBUILD IT. WHEN THE FOUNDATION OF THE TEMPLE IS IN PLACE, THE HIGH PRIEST LEADS THE PEOPLE IN A SERVICE OF WORSHIP AND REJOICING.

O GIVE THANKS UNTO THE LORD, FOR HE IS GOOD. HIS MERCY ENDURETH FOR EVER.

BUT THE SOUND OF REJOICING BRINGS TROUBLE. THE SAMARITANS WHO LIVE NEAR JERUSALEM COME WITH A REQUEST TO HELP BUILD THE TEMPLE.

WE'RE SORRY-- BUT YOU DO NOT WORSHIP AS WE DO, SO WE CANNOT LET YOU HELP US BUILD OUR TEMPLE TO GOD.

SO THEY "CAN'T" LET US HELP THEM BUILD THE TEMPLE! WELL, WE'LL MAKE THEM SORRY THEY EVER CAME BACK TO JERUSALEM TO BUILD ANYTHING.

WHAT DO YOU MEAN?

THE JEWS SOON LEARN WHAT THE SAMARITAN MEANT. ONE DAY WHILE THEY ARE AT WORK AN OFFICER OF KING CYRUS RIDES UP.

BY ORDER OF THE KING, THIS WORK IS TO STOP!

STOP? WHY? IT WAS KING CYRUS HIMSELF WHO TOLD US WE SHOULD RETURN TO JERUSALEM TO REBUILD THE TEMPLE!

UNHAPPILY, THE WORKMEN LAY DOWN THEIR TOOLS AND GO HOME.

FATHER, WHAT COULD HAVE HAPPENED? KING CYRUS SAID...

YES, BUT THE SAMARITANS WROTE HIM THAT WE WERE TRYING TO DESTROY HIS POWER HERE. THE KING IS INVESTIGATING THE CHARGES AND HAS ORDERED WORK ON THE TEMPLE STOPPED.

FORCED TO OBEY, THE JEWS TURN TO WORK ON THEIR HOMES AND GARDENS. SEVERAL YEARS PASS -- CYRUS DIES AND NEW KINGS COME TO THE THRONE IN PERSIA, BUT STILL THE TEMPLE IN JERUSALEM IS NOT COMPLETED. THEN, ONE DAY, THE JEWS ARE APPROACHED BY TWO PROPHETS OF GOD.

HAGGAI, ZECHARIAH! WHAT BRINGS YOU HERE?

WE HAVE NEWS.

A NEW KING, DARIUS, HAS COME TO THE THRONE. LET'S START WORK AGAIN ON THE TEMPLE -- MAYBE HE WON'T STOP US.

KING DARIUS NOT ONLY LETS THE JEWS COMPLETE THE TEMPLE -- HE EVEN ORDERS HIS OFFICERS TO GIVE THEM THE MATERIAL THEY NEED.

SO -- AT LAST -- THE NEW TEMPLE OF GOD IS FINISHED. WITH THANKFUL HEARTS THE PEOPLE OFFER THEIR SACRIFICES AND PRAYERS TO GOD.

SOME YEARS LATER, EZRA, A PRIEST, GAINS PERMISSION FROM THE PERSIAN KING TO GO TO JERUSALEM TO TEACH THE PEOPLE THE LAWS OF GOD. HE TAKES A GROUP OF JEWS WITH HIM. UNDER EZRA JERUSALEM GROWS IN SIZE AND SPIRITUAL STRENGTH, BUT IS STILL WITHOUT WALLS AND SURROUNDED BY HOSTILE NEIGHBORS.

ONE NIGHT, WHILE THE CITY SLEEPS, A STRANGER AND HIS GUARDS RIDE TOWARD JERUSALEM ...

Two Lines of Defense

FROM NEHEMIAH

AT NIGHT, SO THAT NO ONE WILL SEE HIM, A STRANGER TO JERUSALEM RIDES AROUND THE CITY AND EXAMINES THE WALLS.

THE BOOK OF **NEHEMIAH** CONTINUES THE STORY OF THE JEWS' STRUGGLE TO REBUILD JERUSALEM.

THIS CITY COULD BE WIPED OUT IN ONE QUICK ATTACK.

YOU'RE RIGHT, NEHEMIAH. BUT IT MUST HAVE BEEN A GREAT FORTRESS AT ONE TIME. THESE WALLS ARE AS THICK AS ANY WE HAVE IN PERSIA.

THE NEXT DAY NEHEMIAH CALLS ON THE PRIESTS AND RULERS OF THE CITY.

I HAVE EXAMINED THE WALLS OF JERUSALEM. THEY ARE JUST HEAPS OF BROKEN STONE. THE CITY IS DEFENSELESS.

YOU ARE RIGHT, BUT WHY--

WHY HAVE I COME? BECAUSE I, TOO, AM A JEW. AND WHILE I WAS SERVING THE KING OF PERSIA AS HIS CUPBEARER, I LEARNED THAT JERUSALEM WAS WITHOUT ANY DEFENSE. I PRAYED TO GOD-- AND THE KING GAVE ME HIS PERMISSION TO COME HERE AND BUILD UP THE WALLS. ARE YOU WITH ME?

WE ARE-- AND WE'LL START AT ONCE.

THE WORK BEGINS. EVERY ABLE-BODIED MAN AND BOY DOES HIS PART. THE WOMEN HELP... AND SLOWLY THE WALLS BEGIN TO RISE.

BUT SOME OF THE NEIGHBORING COUNTRIES DO NOT WANT TO SEE JERUSALEM PROTECTED.

IF THOSE WALLS ARE FINISHED, THE CITY WILL BE TOO STRONG TO ATTACK. WE MUST STOP IT NOW.

DOWN WITH THE WALLS!

78

Search for a Queen

FROM ESTHER 1: 1—2: 11

THE BOOK OF ESTHER IS THE STORY OF A YOUNG JEWISH WOMAN WHO RISKS HER LIFE TO SAVE HER PEOPLE.

WHEN THE BABYLONIANS CAPTURE JERUSALEM, THEY TAKE THOUSANDS OF JEWS BACK HOME AS CAPTIVES. LATER, WHEN THE PERSIAN KING CONQUERS BABYLON, HE FREES THE JEWS. MANY RETURN TO JERUSALEM, BUT OTHERS REMAIN IN BABYLON AND PERSIA.

AT THIS TIME THE PERSIAN EMPIRE IS THE MOST POWERFUL IN ALL THE WORLD--REACHING FROM INDIA TO ETHIOPIA. ON THE THRONE AT SHUSHAN SITS KING AHASUERUS.

FOR MONTHS THE KING HAS BEEN ENTERTAINING HIGH-RANKING OFFICIALS OF HIS REALM. HOW MUCH LONGER WILL THIS FEASTING GO ON?

UNTIL HE HAS IMPRESSED ALL OF HIS SUBJECTS WITH HIS WEALTH AND POWER.

FINALLY, THE LAST GREAT FEAST IS HELD. AFTER HOURS OF FEASTING, THE DRUNKEN KING GIVES A COMMAND.

BRING QUEEN VASHTI HERE SO THAT ALL OF MY GUESTS MAY SEE HOW BEAUTIFUL SHE IS.

THE MESSAGE IS DELIVERED, BUT...

TELL THE KING THAT I WILL NOT COME TO BE STARED AT BY A GROUP OF DRUNKEN MEN!

SHOCKED BY HIS WIFE'S REFUSAL TO OBEY HIM, THE KING CALLS ON HIS WISE MEN FOR ADVICE.

THIS COULD START TROUBLE THROUGHOUT YOUR WHOLE REALM. IF OTHER WOMEN HEAR OF THIS, THEY WILL THINK THEY CAN DISOBEY THEIR HUSBANDS, TOO. YOUR NOBLES MIGHT TURN AGAINST YOU.

Plot Against the King

FROM ESTHER 2: 11—3: 6

83

84

Revenge!

FROM ESTHER 3: 8—4: 16

ANGERED BECAUSE MORDECAI WILL NOT BOW BEFORE HIM, HAMAN PREPARES HIS REVENGE...

THERE'S A RACE OF PEOPLE IN YOUR KINGDOM, SIR, WHO DO NOT OBEY YOU. FOR YOUR SAFETY, THEY SHOULD BE DESTROYED. GIVE ME PERMISSION TO MAKE A LAW THAT WILL RID PERSIA OF THEM.

YOU ARE A LOYAL MAN, HAMAN. HERE IS MY RING. USE ITS SEAL TO SHOW THAT YOUR LAW IS MY LAW.

HAMAN ACTS AT ONCE...

WRITE THIS DOWN AND SEE THAT EACH GOVERNOR IN THE KINGDOM RECEIVES A COPY OF IT: "EVERY JEW IN PERSIA IS TO BE DESTROYED ON THE 13TH DAY OF THE 12TH MONTH. THOSE WHO KILL THE JEWS MAY KEEP AS REWARDS ALL THE MONEY AND GOODS OF THE JEWS THEY KILL."

THE ORDERS ARE WRITTEN AND DELIVERED. THROUGHOUT THE KINGDOM JEWISH FAMILIES ARE TERRIFIED...

WHY? WHY? WE HAVE DONE, NO WRONG!

AND WHEREVER WE GO THERE'S A PRICE ON OUR HEADS!

WHEN MORDECAI HEARS THE ORDERS HE DRESSES IN CLOTHES OF MOURNING AND POURS ASHES OVER HIS HEAD TO SHOW HIS GRIEF...

FROM HER PALACE WINDOW ESTHER SEES THAT SOMETHING IS WRONG.

FIND OUT WHAT IS TROUBLING MORDECAI.

THE QUEEN ASKS WHY I MOURN? DOESN'T SHE KNOW THAT HAMAN'S ORDER MEANS DEATH TO EVERY JEW IN PERSIA? SHOW THIS TO HER-- TELL HER SHE MUST GO TO THE KING AND ASK HIM TO SPARE THE JEWS.

THE FRIGHTENED SERVANT CARRIES THE MESSAGE TO ESTHER.

I GO TO SEE THE KING? MORDECAI KNOWS THAT ANYONE WHO APPEARS BEFORE THE KING WITHOUT BEING INVITED IS SUBJECT TO DEATH. AND I HAVE NOT BEEN CALLED TO SEE THE KING FOR THIRTY DAYS.

NOW, MORE FRIGHTENED THAN EVER, THE SERVANT REPORTS BACK TO MORDECAI.

TELL THE QUEEN I UNDERSTAND HER FEAR. BUT TELL HER, TOO, THAT PERHAPS GOD RAISED HER UP TO THE PALACE FOR SUCH A TIME AS THIS.

AFTER RECEIVING MORDECAI'S LAST MESSAGE, ESTHER PREPARES TO GO TO THE KING.

BRING THE ROYAL ROBES — I WILL GO LOOKING AS A QUEEN SHOULD.

NO! NO! THIS COULD MEAN YOUR DEATH!

87

A Queen Risks Her Life

FROM ESTHER 5: 1—6: 10

QUEEN ESTHER BREAKS A LAW BY APPEARING UNINVITED BEFORE THE KING--AN ACT PUNISHABLE BY DEATH. BUT THE LIVES OF HER PEOPLE, THE JEWS, ARE IN DANGER, AND SHE IS THE ONLY ONE WHO MAY BE ABLE TO SAVE THEM.

ESTHER! WHAT DOES SHE WANT THAT SHE WOULD RISK HER LIFE TO GET?

SURPRISED AS HE IS BY HER SUDDEN APPEARANCE, THE KING IS PLEASED AT THE SIGHT OF HIS BEAUTIFUL QUEEN. HE HOLDS OUT HIS SCEPTOR TO SHOW THAT SHE IS FORGIVEN, AND ASKS WHAT SHE WANTS.

I ASK THAT YOU AND HAMAN COME TO A DINNER THAT I SHALL PREPARE FOR YOU.

THE KING ACCEPTS. SO DOES HAMAN -- WHO IS OVERJOYED UNTIL HE LEAVES THE PALACE.

THAT STUBBORN JEW -- HE STILL WON'T BOW BEFORE ME! WELL, HE'LL SOON BE DEAD WITH ALL THE OTHER JEWS.

AT HOME HAMAN COMPLAINS THAT MORDECAI HAS INSULTED HIM.

DON'T STAND FOR IT, HAMAN. BUILD A GALLOWS AND TELL THE KING YOU WANT MORDECAI HANGED. THEN YOU CAN ENJOY YOUR DINNER WITH THE QUEEN.

I'LL DO IT! I'LL HAVE THE GALLOWS MADE AND GO TO SEE THE KING EARLY IN THE MORNING.

BUT THAT NIGHT THE KING CANNOT SLEEP. HE CALLS FOR A SCRIBE TO READ TO HIM FROM THE RECORDS OF THE KINGDOM. WHEN THE READING REACHES THE STORY OF MORDECAI, THE KING INTERRUPTS.

STOP! WHAT REWARD DID HE RECEIVE FOR SAVING MY LIFE?

NONE, MY LORD.

AT THAT MOMENT HAMAN ENTERS THE COURT AND IS BROUGHT BEFORE THE KING.

HAMAN, YOU'RE JUST THE MAN I WANTED TO SEE. WHAT SHALL I DO TO HONOR A MAN WHO HAS PLEASED ME?

I KNEW THE KING WOULD RECOGNIZE MY SERVICES.

LET HIM WEAR ONE OF YOUR ROBES -- AND RIDE YOUR HORSE. THEN HAVE ONE OF YOUR NOBLES LEAD HIM THROUGH THE CITY TELLING EVERYONE THAT THIS IS THE WAY THE KING HONORS THOSE WHO PLEASE HIM.

GOOD! GET THE ROBE AND THE HORSE AND DO EXACTLY AS YOU HAVE SUGGESTED -- FOR MORDECAI.

MORDECAI! BUT I -- YES-- SIR!

The Unchangeable Law

FROM ESTHER 6: 11—10

ANGRY AND HUMILIATED, HAMAN IS FORCED TO PERFORM FOR HIS ENEMY, MORDECAI, THE CEREMONY THAT HE HAD PLANNED FOR HIMSELF...

THE CEREMONY OVER, HAMAN COVERS HIS HEAD IN SHAME AND HURRIES HOME TO TELL HIS FAMILY.

THIS LOOKS BAD FOR YOU, HAMAN.

ALL IS NOT LOST! THE KING HAS SIGNED AN ORDER TO KILL THE JEWS, AND NOT EVEN HE CAN CHANGE IT! NOW I MUST DRESS TO GO TO QUEEN ESTHER'S DINNER. AT LEAST SHE RECOGNIZES ME!

LATER AT THE PALACE.

QUEEN ESTHER, WHEN YOU DARED TO COME TO THE THRONE ROOM I THINK YOU WANTED A GREATER FAVOR THAN TO ASK ME TO DINNER. DIDN'T YOU?

YES, MY LORD, I DID.

WHAT IS IT? I'LL GRANT WHATEVER YOU ASK.

I ASK FOR THE LIFE OF MYSELF AND MY PEOPLE. BY THE CRUEL PLAN OF A CERTAIN MAN WE ARE TO BE PUT TO DEATH.

PUT **YOU** TO DEATH? WHO WOULD DARE DO SUCH A THING?

HAMAN!

Now, FOR THE FIRST TIME THE KING KNOWS THAT HIS WIFE IS JEWISH, AND THAT HAMAN TRICKED HIM INTO SIGNING HER DEATH WARRANT. IN ANGER THE KING LEAVES THE ROOM.

QUEEN ESTHER! I'LL DO ANYTHING YOU SAY-- ONLY SPARE ME! SPARE ME!

THE KING'S SERVANT KNOWS THAT HAMAN IS DOOMED TO DIE AND HE COVERS THE MAN'S HEAD WITH A CLOTH.

93

94

The Test of a Man

FROM JOB 1—2: 9

JOB, THE 18TH BOOK OF THE BIBLE, DESCRIBES THE TESTING OF A MAN'S FAITH IN GOD.

JOB IS THE RICHEST MAN IN UZ, A COUNTRY NEAR PALESTINE. AS FAR AS HE CAN LOOK IN EVERY DIRECTION HE SEES FLOCKS, HERDS, AND SERVANTS -- ALL HIS. ONE DAY A FRIEND ASKS HIM A QUESTION EVERYONE IN UZ HAS BEEN WONDERING ABOUT FOR A LONG TIME.

HOW DO YOU ACCOUNT FOR YOUR GREAT SUCCESS, JOB?

ALL MY LIFE I HAVE LOVED AND TRIED TO SERVE GOD. AND I PRAY THAT MY CHILDREN WILL DO SO, TOO.

ON HIS WAY HOME THE MAN TELLS HIS FRIENDS HOW JOB EXPLAINS HIS GREAT WEALTH.

YES, JOB **IS** A GOOD MAN.

AND HE HAS CERTAINLY BEEN REWARDED FOR HIS GOODNESS.

THAT EVENING JOB JOINS HIS FAMILY AT THE MAIN MEAL OF THE DAY.

THE CHIEF SHEPHERD TELLS ME OUR FLOCKS HAVE BEEN INCREASED BY A THOUSAND LAMBS. SURELY THERE IS NO MAN IN THE WHOLE WORLD MORE FORTUNATE THAN I — FLOCKS, HERDS, AND BEST OF ALL, A LOVING FAMILY.

GOD, TOO, IS PLEASED. AND ONE DAY HE TELLS SATAN WHAT A GOOD MAN JOB IS. BUT SATAN ARGUES BACK: "JOB IS GOOD ONLY BECAUSE YOU HAVE BEEN GOOD TO HIM. LET ME GIVE HIM SOME TROUBLE; THEN WE'LL SEE HOW GOOD HE IS." SO GOD LETS SATAN TEST JOB.

FIRST, RAIDERS ATTACK JOB'S HERDS, STEALING THE ANIMALS AND KILLING THE HERDSMEN.

THEN, LIGHTNING STRIKES THE FLOCK, KILLING THE SHEEP AND THE SHEPHERDS.

AND FINALLY, A STORM RIPS DOWN THE HOUSE IN WHICH HIS SONS AND DAUGHTERS ARE FEASTING. ALL ARE KILLED.

96

JOB IS STUNNED BY THE NEWS OF THE FIRST DISASTER, BUT WHEN HE LEARNS OF THE DEATH OF HIS CHILDREN, HE IS GRIEF STRICKEN. FOLLOWING THE CUSTOM OF HIS PEOPLE, HE SHOWS HIS SORROW BY TEARING HIS ROBE AND SHAVING HIS HEAD. BUT HE DOES NOT TURN AWAY FROM GOD.

THE LORD GAVE MY CHILDREN TO ME AND THE LORD HAS TAKEN THEM AWAY-- BLESSED BE THE NAME OF THE LORD.

GOD IS PLEASED WITH JOB'S LOYALTY. BUT AGAIN SATAN ARGUES: A MAN WILL DO ANYTHING TO SAVE HIS OWN LIFE. BRING DISASTER TO JOB HIMSELF, AND HE WILL CURSE YOU. SO GOD LETS SATAN CONTINUE THE TESTING.

JOB! WHAT IS THE MATTER?

LOOK AT THESE UGLY SORES. I'M COVERED WITH THEM! AND THE PAIN IS ALMOST MORE THAN I CAN STAND.

BECAUSE OF HIS ILLNESS, JOB IS NOW AN OUTCAST. IN DESPAIR HE WANDERS OUT OF THE CITY AND FALLS ON A HEAP OF ASHES. FINDING JOB IN THIS DISGRACEFUL CONDITION IS TOO MUCH FOR HIS WIFE. IN BITTERNESS AND ANGER OVER ALL THEY HAVE LOST, SHE TURNS ON HIM.

WHAT GOOD IS YOUR FAITH IN GOD DOING YOU NOW? WHY DON'T YOU CURSE HIM FOR ALL THE TROUBLE HE HAS LET COME TO YOU? DEATH WOULD BE NO WORSE THAN THIS.

OUR BIBLE IN PICTURES
God's Answer
FROM JOB 2: 10— 42

COVERED WITH PAINFUL SORES, JOB, ONCE THE RICHEST MAN IN ALL THE LAND, IS NOW AN OUTCAST. HIS WIFE IS BITTER ABOUT THEIR TROUBLES AND TRIES TO GET HIM TO BLAME GOD FOR THEM, BUT JOB WILL NOT. AFTER A WHILE SOME OF HIS FRIENDS GO TO SEE HIM.

I HEARD JOB WAS SICK, BUT I NEVER THOUGHT HIS ILLNESS WAS AS BAD AS THIS!

WHAT DO YOU SUPPOSE HE DID TO DESERVE SUCH MISERY?

WHEN THEY REACH JOB THEY FIND HIM IN SUCH AGONY THAT THEY WAIT FOR HIM TO SPEAK FIRST.

OH, I WISH I HAD NEVER BEEN BORN!

DON'T SAY THAT. EVERYONE SINS AND MUST BE PUNISHED FOR IT. DID YOU THINK YOU COULD GO THROUGH LIFE WITHOUT ANY TROUBLE?

99

The World's Greatest Poetry

FROM PSALMS, PROVERBS, ECCLESIASTES, SONG OF SOLOMON

PSALMS IS A COLLECTION OF 150 SONGS AND POEMS. THEY EXPRESS THE FEELINGS OF THE HEBREW PEOPLE TOWARD GOD AS THEY TURNED TO HIM ABOUT THE MANY PROBLEMS AND EVENTS OF THEIR LIVES. IT IS ONE OF THE BEST-LOVED BOOKS IN THE OLD TESTAMENT; JESUS AND THE NEW TESTAMENT WRITERS QUOTED FROM IT MANY TIMES.

DAVID, THE SHEPHERD BOY WHO BECAME ISRAEL'S GREATEST KING, WROTE MANY OF THE PSALMS AND USED THEM IN THE SERVICES HE ORGANIZED FOR THE WORSHIP OF GOD.

THE BOOK OF **PROVERBS** IS A COLLECTION OF WISE SAYINGS, TEACHING PEOPLE THE RIGHT WAY TO ACT TO BE HAPPY. MOST OF THE PROVERBS WERE SPOKEN BY KING SOLOMON WHO, WHEN HE BECAME KING OF ISRAEL, PRAYED TO GOD FOR WISDOM TO RULE HIS PEOPLE.

A SOFT ANSWER TURNETH AWAY WRATH: BUT GRIEVOUS WORDS STIR UP ANGER.

ECCLESIASTES IS THE STORY OF SOLOMON'S SEARCH FOR AN ANSWER TO THE QUESTION: WHAT MAKES LIFE WORTH LIVING?

EVEN WITH ALL HIS WEALTH AND WISDOM, SOLOMON REALIZES THAT SOMETHING IS LACKING IN HIS LIFE.

102

HE STUDIES HOW OTHER PEOPLE LIVE -- AND FINDS THAT THE WORKERS IN THE FIELDS ARE AS HAPPY IN THEIR WAY OF LIFE AS HE -- WITH MONEY AND WISDOM -- IS IN HIS.

THE HAPPINESS THAT MAKES LIFE WORTH LIVING, HE DISCOVERS, COMES TO EACH MAN -- NOT FROM OUTWARD POSSESSIONS, BUT FROM TRUSTING GOD AND MAKING USE OF GOD'S GIFTS TO HIM.

THE BOOK ENDS WITH THIS ADVICE TO YOUNG PEOPLE: REMEMBER NOW THY CREATOR IN THE DAYS OF THY YOUTH...FEAR GOD, AND KEEP HIS COMMANDMENTS.

THE SONG OF SOLOMON IS A BOOK OF POETRY TELLING THE LOVE OF SOLOMON FOR A BEAUTIFUL MAIDEN. THE HEBREWS SAW IN THIS BOOK A PICTURE OF THE LOVE OF GOD FOR HIS PEOPLE.

A Man with a Message

FROM THE BOOK OF ISAIAH

THINGS SEEMED TO BE GOING WELL IN THE LAND OF JUDAH, BUT TROUBLE WAS ON THE WAY. IN THEIR HEARTS THE PEOPLE WERE TURNING AWAY FROM GOD. THE RICH WERE CHEATING THE POOR. AND ALTHOUGH THE WALLS OF JERUSALEM WERE STRONG, THERE WAS ALWAYS THE DANGER OF INVASION BY AN ENEMY. IN THIS TIME OF NEED, GOD SENT A YOUNG MAN WITH A MESSAGE. HE WAS ISAIAH, ONE OF THE GREATEST OF THE HEBREW PROPHETS.

HOLY, HOLY, HOLY, IS THE LORD GOD OF HOSTS.

THE CALL TO BECOME A PROPHET OF GOD COMES TO ISAIAH WHEN HE IS WORSHIPING IN THE TEMPLE. AS HE PRAYS, HE SEES A GLORIOUS VISION.

O GOD, I AM NOT WORTHY TO BE IN THY PRESENCE. I AM A SINFUL MAN IN A SINFUL NATION.

AN ANGEL TOUCHES ISAIAH'S LIPS WITH A COAL OF FIRE AND SAYS, "YOUR SIN IS TAKEN AWAY." THEN ISAIAH HEARS GOD ASK: "WHOM SHALL I SEND TO SPEAK TO THIS SINFUL NATION?"

HERE I AM; SEND ME.

DON'T YOU SEE -- JUST AS YOU CALL BACK THE MONEY YOU LEND, SO WILL GOD CALL BACK THE LIFE HE HAS LOANED TO YOU? THEN YOU'LL BE JUDGED FOR WHAT YOU HAVE DONE.

I'LL WORRY ABOUT THAT LATER.

FOR MORE THAN FIFTY YEARS ISAIAH PLEADS WITH HIS PEOPLE TO DESTROY THEIR IDOLS AND WORSHIP GOD. BUT ONLY A FEW LISTEN. HE WARNS THE KINGS OF WHAT WILL HAPPEN IF THEY DISOBEY GOD, BUT THE KINGS IGNORE THE WARNINGS. AT LAST ISAIAH PROPHESIES DESTRUCTION...

BECAUSE JUDAH HAS TURNED AWAY FROM GOD, IT WILL BE DESTROYED AND ITS PEOPLE CARRIED AWAY AS CAPTIVES.

IS THERE NO HOPE FOR GOD'S PEOPLE?

YES, GOD WILL SEND A DELIVERER TO SAVE ALL WHO BELIEVE IN HIM. AND HIS NAME SHALL BE CALLED WONDERFUL, COUNSELLOR, THE MIGHTY GOD... THE PRINCE OF PEACE.

SEVEN HUNDRED YEARS AFTER ISAIAH MAKES THE PROPHECY, IT COMES TRUE WHEN CHRIST, THE SAVIOR OF ALL MANKIND, IS BORN.

OUR BIBLE IN PICTURES

A Call from God

FROM JEREMIAH 1; II KINGS 22: 1—23: 29

"JUDAH WILL BE DESTROYED FOR DISOBEYING GOD!" THE PROPHET ISAIAH WARNED. BUT THE PEOPLE OF JUDAH IGNORED THE WARNING AND CONTINUED THEIR MAD RUSH TOWARDS RUIN. THEN GOD CALLED ANOTHER PROPHET NAMED JEREMIAH TO SOUND THE ALARM AGAIN.

IT'S AN EXCITING DAY FOR JEREMIAH WHEN HE GOES TO JERUSALEM WITH HIS FATHER TO SEE JUDAH'S NEW KING.

LONG LIVE KING JOSIAH!

WHY! HE'S JUST ABOUT MY AGE! I WONDER WHAT IT WOULD BE LIKE TO HAVE SUCH AN IMPORTANT JOB.

A FEW YEARS LATER JEREMIAH FINDS OUT, FOR GOD CALLS HIM TO AN EVEN GREATER TASK-- TO BECOME SPOKESMAN FOR HIM.

O GOD--I DON'T KNOW HOW TO SPEAK SO THAT PEOPLE WILL LISTEN. I'M TOO YOUNG FOR SUCH A BIG JOB.

108

HE SOON FINDS OUT-- WHEN HE TELLS THE PRIESTS IN HIS OWN TOWN THAT JUDAH WILL BE DESTROYED BECAUSE THE PEOPLE HAVE TURNED FROM GOD TO WORSHIP IDOLS.

WHO IS THIS YOUNG UPSTART TO TELL US HOW TO LIVE?

LET'S GET RID OF HIM BEFORE HE STARTS TROUBLE.

SO, TO SAVE HIS LIFE, JEREMIAH IS FORCED TO LEAVE HIS HOME TOWN AND GO TO JERUSALEM.

KING JOSIAH LOVES AND WORSHIPS GOD; HE WILL HELP ME TRY TO SAVE JUDAH.

FOR SEVERAL YEARS JEREMIAH AND THE KING WORK TOGETHER TO DESTROY IDOL WORSHIP. THEN, ONE DAY, JEREMIAH HEARS SOME FRIGHTENING NEWS.

THE ASSYRIAN EMPIRE IS CRACKING UP. EGYPT IS MARCHING NORTH TO GRAB WHAT'S LEFT. KING JOSIAH DECLARES HE WILL STOP THE EGYPTIAN ARMY FROM MARCHING THROUGH JUDAH.

STOP EGYPT? WHY, IT'S ONE OF THE STRONGEST COUNTRIES IN THE WORLD! THE KING IS MAKING A BIG MISTAKE.

MEDITERRANEAN

EGYPT

JUDAH

ASSYRIAN EMPIRE

BUT KING JOSIAH LEADS HIS SOLDIERS OUT OF THE GATES OF JERUSALEM — AND INTO THE PATH OF THE ONCOMING EGYPTIAN ARMY.

OUR BIBLE IN PICTURES

The Broken Vase

FROM JEREMIAH 18—20: 2; II KINGS 23: 30-37

KING JOSIAH IS KILLED AS HE ATTEMPTS TO DEFEAT THE EGYPTIANS. NOW HIS SON, JEHOIAKIM, SITS ON THE THRONE OF JUDAH AS A PUPPET RULER FOR EGYPT. AT ONCE THE IDOL WORSHIPERS BEGIN THEIR CAMPAIGN AGAINST GOD AND HIS PROPHET, JEREMIAH.

O KING, YOUR FATHER ORDERED US NOT TO WORSHIP ANY GOD BUT JEHOVAH. AND WHAT HAPPENED? JUDAH IS NO LONGER A FREE COUNTRY. JOIN US IN WORSHIPING OUR GODS SO THAT JUDAH WILL BECOME STRONG-- LIKE OUR NEIGHBORS.

JEHOIAKIM AGREES--AND IN SPITE OF JEREMIAH'S WARNINGS, MANY OF THE PEOPLE FOLLOW THE KING'S LEAD.

GO AWAY, JEREMIAH. NOBODY WANTS TO LISTEN TO YOUR FAR-FETCHED STORIES ABOUT JUDAH BEING DESTROYED!

JEREMIAH SEARCHES FOR A WAY TO SHOW HIS PEOPLE WHAT WILL HAPPEN TO JUDAH -- AND WHY. HE FINDS HIS ANSWER ONE DAY WHEN HE VISITS A POTTER'S SHOP.

THE VASE -- YOU'RE TURNING IT BACK INTO A LUMP OF CLAY!

YES, IT DIDN'T TURN OUT TO BE A GOOD VASE. THE ONLY WAY I CAN MAKE A GOOD VASE NOW IS TO START OVER.

JEREMIAH CALLS THE PRIESTS AND THE CHIEF MEN OF JERUSALEM TO GO TO THE CITY DUMP WITH HIM.

DON'T YOU SEE -- JUDAH IS LIKE THIS VASE. GOD WAS SHAPING IT INTO A GOOD NATION, BUT IT DISOBEYED HIM AND BECAME EVIL. NOW IT CAN NO LONGER SERVE GOD'S PURPOSE FOR IT.

SO JUDAH WILL BE DESTROYED JUST LIKE THIS VASE.

111

IN THE TEMPLE, JEREMIAH PREACHES THE SAME WARNING.

PASHUR, IF THE PEOPLE LISTEN TO JEREMIAH, THEY MAY TURN AGAINST US.

I'LL HANDLE THIS.

AT PASHUR'S COMMAND THE TEMPLE GUARDS SEIZE JEREMIAH.

GIVE HIM 39 LASHES--AND THEN PUT HIM IN THE STOCKS!

THERE! MAYBE THIS WILL TEACH YOU NOT TO STIR UP THE PEOPLE!

OUR BIBLE IN PICTURES
Surrender
FROM JEREMIAH 20—36

BECAUSE JEREMIAH HAS DARED TELL THE PEOPLE THAT JUDAH WILL BE DESTROYED FOR ITS WICKEDNESS, THE PRIESTS HAVE HIM BEATEN AND PLACED IN STOCKS. WHEN HE IS RELEASED, A YOUNG SCRIBE, BARUCH, OFFERS TO HELP HIM.

COME WITH ME AND GET SOME REST.

REST? THERE'S TOO MUCH TO DO, AND TOO LITTLE TIME.

JEREMIAH IS RIGHT-- THERE IS LITTLE TIME. NEWS OF A GREAT BATTLE IS ALREADY SPREADING THROUGHOUT JERUSALEM...

THE BABYLONIANS HAVE DEFEATED EGYPT!

WE'VE BEEN UNDER EGYPT'S CONTROL-- WHAT'S GOING TO HAPPEN TO US NOW?

113

JUDAH DOESN'T HAVE LONG TO WAIT FOR ITS ANSWER. BABYLON ATTACKS JERUSALEM, AND KING JEHOIAKIM IS FORCED TO SURRENDER.

YOU MAY REMAIN ON THE THRONE, JEHOIAKIM, BUT NOW YOU MUST PAY TRIBUTE MONEY TO ME. AND TO SEE THAT YOU DO, I'LL TAKE YOUR BEST PRINCES AS HOSTAGES.

WITHIN DAYS ALL JERUSALEM SADLY WATCHES ITS FINEST YOUNG MEN BEING MARCHED AWAY.

KNOWING THAT THE DOWNFALL OF JUDAH IS NOT FAR OFF, JEREMIAH DICTATES ALL OF THE MESSAGES HE HAS RECEIVED FROM GOD.

THE PEOPLE MUST BE TOLD THAT GOD IS ALLOWING JUDAH TO BE PUNISHED FOR ITS SINS.

THEN--BECAUSE HE IS NOT ALLOWED IN THE TEMPLE--JEREMIAH ASKS BARUCH TO READ GOD'S WORD TO THE PEOPLE.

WE MUST SEE THAT THE KING LEARNS ABOUT THIS.

115

OUR BIBLE IN PICTURES

Rebellion

FROM II KINGS 24: 1-6;
JEREMIAH 27; 28: 1-12; 37: 1-10

KING JEHOIAKIM'S REVOLT AGAINST BABYLON IS WELL UNDER WAY -- WHEN -- SUDDENLY -- HE DIES. HIS SON, JEHOIACHIN, COMES TO THE THRONE AND PLEDGES TO UPHOLD HIS FATHER'S STAND FOR JUDAH'S FREEDOM. IN SPITE OF THE KING'S OPPOSITION, JEREMIAH REPEATS HIS WARNING...

JUDAH MADE AN AGREEMENT WITH BABYLON, AND JUDAH WILL BE PUNISHED FOR BREAKING IT.

JEREMIAH KNOWS THAT THE TIME IS SHORT, BUT HE CONTINUES TO PLEAD WITH HIS PEOPLE TO STOP THE REVOLT. HIS PLEAS ARE IGNORED. THEN ONE DAY...

THE BABYLONIANS ARE COMING!

WITH FULL FORCE THE ARMY OF BABYLON STORMS THE WALLS OF JERUSALEM.

YOUNG KING JEHOIACHIN, WHO HAS RULED THREE MONTHS, IS FORCED TO SURRENDER TO KING NEBUCHADNEZZAR.

THIS TIME I WILL TAKE YOUR TREASURES, YOUR NOBLES, YOUR SKILLED WORKERS **AND** YOUR KING. LET THIS BE A LESSON TO YOU WHO ARE LEFT!

SO JEREMIAH'S PROPHECY COMES TRUE! THE TEMPLE TREASURES ARE LOOTED, THE KING AND 10,000 OF JUDAH'S ABLEST MEN ARE LED AWAY. PRINCE ZEDEKIAH IS MADE KING-- **AFTER** HE PROMISES LOYALTY TO BABYLON.

FOR A FEW YEARS KING ZEDEKIAH PAYS TRIBUTE TO BABYLON. THEN, IN SPITE OF JEREMIAH'S WARNINGS, HE BEGINS TO LISTEN TO SOME HOT-HEADED YOUNG ADVISERS IN HIS COURT.

WHAT DO **WE** GET FROM THE MONEY PAID TO BABYLON?

WELL-- WE GET PEACE.

PEACE--BUT NOT FREEDOM! MAYBE THE EGYPTIANS WILL HELP US-- THEY HATE BABYLON, TOO.

LET ME THINK ABOUT IT.

WHEN JEREMIAH LEARNS THAT THERE IS TALK OF ANOTHER REVOLT, HE PUTS AN OX YOKE ON HIS SHOULDERS AND WALKS THROUGH THE STREETS.

WHAT'S THE MEANING OF THIS?

BABYLON HAS STRUCK TWICE, AND IT WILL STRIKE AGAIN. THE NEXT TIME IT WILL DESTROY JERUSALEM. JUDAH'S ONLY HOPE OF SURVIVAL IS TO WEAR THE YOKE OF BABYLON AS I AM WEARING THIS ONE.

I'LL SHOW YOU WHAT TO DO WITH THE YOKE OF BABYLON. BREAK IT!

DURING ALL OF THIS TIME, EGYPT KEEPS AN ANXIOUS EYE ON THE GROWING TENSIONS IN JUDAH. AT THE RIGHT MOMENT IT SENDS AN AMBASSADOR TO KING ZEDEKIAH.

BABYLON IS YOUR ENEMY AS WELL AS OURS. ALONE, NEITHER ONE OF US CAN DEFEAT THEM, BUT--

TOGETHER WE CAN! AND WE WILL!

118

A Prophecy Comes True

FROM JEREMIAH 38: 7—43: 7

JEREMIAH IS TAKEN BACK TO PRISON... THE SIEGE GOES ON, BUT AT THE END OF 30 MONTHS...

THE BABYLONIANS HAVE BROKEN THROUGH THE WALL!

JERUSALEM WILL BE DESTROYED! BUT IT WILL RISE AGAIN... AND SOMEDAY GOD'S COMMANDMENTS WILL BE WRITTEN IN THE HEARTS OF MEN WHO CHOOSE TO OBEY GOD. THEY WILL LIVE TOGETHER IN PEACE.

KING ZEDEKIAH TRIES TO ESCAPE, BUT IS CAPTURED AND BLINDED. THE KING, JEREMIAH, AND MOST OF THE ABLE-BODIED PEOPLE ARE CAPTURED TO BE TAKEN TO BABYLON.

BUT IN THE CAPTIVE CAMP AT RAMAH...

THE KING OF BABYLON HAS LEARNED THAT YOU TRIED TO KEEP YOUR COUNTRY FROM REBELLING AGAINST HIM, SO HE HAS SENT ORDERS TO SET YOU FREE.

THANK GOD! NOW I CAN HELP THE PEOPLE WHO HAVE BEEN LEFT IN ISRAEL WITHOUT A LEADER.

ABOUT A MONTH AFTER JERUSALEM IS TAKEN, A BABYLONIAN OFFICER RETURNS, TAKES MORE CAPTIVES, AND THEN SETS FIRE TO THE CITY.

THE FIRE RAGES FOR DAYS -- UNTIL THE ONCE-PROUD CAPITAL OF JUDAH BECOMES A HEAP OF SMOULDERING RUINS.

THE BABYLONIANS SET UP HEADQUARTERS AT MIZPAH AND APPOINT AN ISRAELITE TO ACT AS GOVERNOR. JEREMIAH JOINS HIM -- AND BECOMES HIS ADVISER.

TOGETHER WE'LL ENCOURAGE THE PEOPLE TO BUILD UP THEIR HOMES AND REPLANT THEIR VINEYARDS AND FIELDS.

SOMEDAY THE CAPTIVES WILL RETURN-- AND JUDAH WILL BECOME A NATION AGAIN.

BUT BEFORE THE GOVERNOR'S DREAM CAN COME TRUE HE IS MURDERED BY SOME ISRAELITES WHO ARE JEALOUS OF HIS POWER IN THE COUNTRY. FEARFUL THAT BABYLON WILL BLAME ALL ISRAEL FOR THE MURDER, A GROUP OF PEOPLE GO TO JEREMIAH...

WE WANT TO GO TO EGYPT-- WHERE THERE IS PEACE AND PLENTY TO EAT.

YOU WILL FIND NEITHER PEACE NOR PLENTY IN EGYPT. STAY HERE -- THE BABYLONIANS WILL NOT HURT YOU.

BUT THE PEOPLE DO NOT BELIEVE JEREMIAH. THEY FLEE TO EGYPT, FORCING HIM TO GO WITH THEM. AND THERE, UNTIL HE DIES, JEREMIAH TRIES TO LEAD HIS PEOPLE BACK TO GOD.

THE GRIEF OF THE JEWS OVER THE DESTRUCTION OF JERUSALEM IS EXPRESSED IN A GROUP OF POEMS FOUND IN THE

BOOK OF LAMENTATIONS

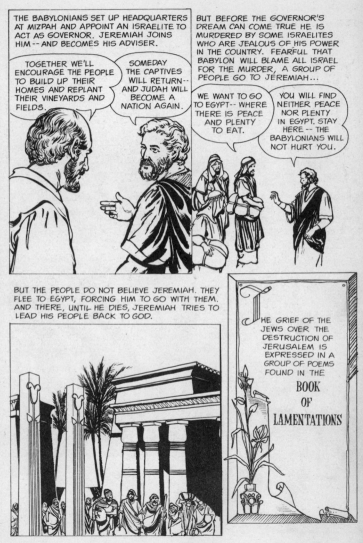

Ten Thousand Captives

FROM EZEKIEL 1

TO UNDERSTAND THE **BOOK OF EZEKIEL**, YOU MUST TURN BACK THE PAGES OF TIME -- TO BABYLON'S SECOND SIEGE OF JERUSALEM. JERUSALEM SURRENDERED AND WAS FORCED TO WATCH 10,000 OF ITS PEOPLE MARCHED AWAY AS CAPTIVES. BUT GOD DID NOT FORSAKE THESE CAPTIVES -- HE CALLED ONE OF THEM, A YOUNG PRIEST NAMED EZEKIEL, TO SERVE AS HIS PROPHET AMONG THE EXILES IN BABYLON.

FRIGHTENED AND WEARY FROM THE 900 MILE MARCH, THE 10,000 CAPTIVES FROM JUDAH REACH THE GATES OF BABYLON, THE GIANT CITY OF THEIR CONQUERORS.

ONLY GOD KNOWS WHAT WILL HAPPEN TO US NOW.

EZEKIEL, A YOUNG PRIEST, AND HIS WIFE ARE AMONG THE CAPTIVES WONDERING WHERE THEY WILL LIVE.

WHERE ARE WE GOING?

TO TEL-ABIB, ON THE CHEBAR CANAL. YOU CAN BUILD YOUR HOMES THERE AND WORK THE FIELDS.

IN THE MONTHS THAT FOLLOW, EZEKIEL WORKS HARD TO MAKE A LIVING IN THE NEW LAND.

IT IS NOT AS BAD AS I FEARED. WE ARE WELL TREATED--AND WE ARE TOGETHER.

YES. WE MAY HAVE TO STAY HERE THE REST OF OUR LIVES, BUT GOD IS WITH US WHEREVER WE ARE.

BUT NOT ALL OF THE CAPTIVES FEEL THE SAME WAY.

WHAT DO YOU THINK OF EZEKIEL PLANTING TREES AND PLANNING TO BUILD A HOUSE? LOOKS AS IF HE INTENDS TO STAY IN BABYLONIA.

HE'S WASTING HIS TIME. WE'LL BE ON OUR WAY HOME IN A COUPLE OF YEARS.

WHEN THIS NEWS REACHES GOD'S PROPHET, JEREMIAH, IN JUDAH, HE WRITES A LETTER TO THE CAPTIVES.

JEREMIAH SAYS IT IS GOD'S WILL THAT WE STAY HERE. WE SHOULD BUILD HOMES AND WORK FOR THE GOOD OF OUR NEW COUNTRY. WE WILL BE HERE FOR SEVENTY YEARS.

DID YOU HEAR THAT, EZEKIEL? SEVENTY YEARS -- I DON'T BELIEVE IT!

JEREMIAH SPEAKS THE WILL OF GOD.

EZEKIEL SHOWS HIS FAITH BY BUILDING A HOUSE.

WE'LL MAKE A LARGE COURTYARD -- BIG ENOUGH TO INVITE PEOPLE HERE TO WORSHIP GOD. I USED TO THINK THAT WE COULD WORSHIP GOD ONLY IN THE TEMPLE IN JERUSALEM, BUT NOW I KNOW WE CAN WORSHIP HIM ANYWHERE.

OUR BIBLE IN PICTURES
A Message of Hope
FROM EZEKIEL 1—48

IN A STRANGE AND BEAUTIFUL VISION GOD CALLED EZEKIEL TO BE HIS PROPHET AND SPEAK TO THE PEOPLE OF JERUSALEM WHO ARE CAPTIVES IN BABYLON. FOLLOWING GOD'S COMMAND, EZEKIEL DRAWS THE OUTLINE OF A CITY, AND AROUND IT PLACES AN ENEMY CAMP.

THIS IS JERUSALEM. IT HAS TURNED FROM GOD TO WORSHIP IDOLS AND FOR THIS--

IT WILL BE DESTROYED!

NO! NO! NOT JERUSALEM! NOT OUR HOLY CITY!

EZEKIEL KEEPS WARNING THE PEOPLE THAT JERUSALEM WILL BE DESTROYED, BUT THEY REFUSE TO BELIEVE HIM. THEN -- SUDDENLY -- EZEKIEL'S WIFE DIES. BUT THE PROPHET SHOWS NO OUTWARD SIGN OF GRIEF.

WE MOURN FOR YOUR WIFE, EZEKIEL. WHY DO YOU NOT MOURN FOR THE ONE YOU LOVED?

YES, I LOVED HER VERY MUCH. BUT GOD HAS COMMANDED ME NOT TO SHOW MY GRIEF, AS A SIGN THAT YOU ARE NOT TO SHOW YOUR GRIEF WHEN JERUSALEM FALLS.

BUT THE PEOPLE WILL NOT GIVE UP BELIEVING THAT JERUSALEM WILL BE STANDING -- STRONG AND BEAUTIFUL -- WAITING FOR THEIR RETURN. ONE DAY A MAN STAGGERS WEARILY INTO THEIR MIDST...

WHAT BRINGS YOU HERE?

I'M FROM WHAT WAS JERUSALEM.

129

130

Captives in Babylon

FROM DANIEL 1—2: 13

THE STORY OF WHAT HAPPENED TO A ROYAL CAPTIVE FROM JUDAH BEGINS WHEN DANIEL AND HIS THREE FRIENDS—SHADRACH, MESHACH, AND ABEDNEGO—ENTER THE CITY OF BABYLON AT THE END OF THEIR 900 MILE MARCH FROM JERUSALEM.

WHAT DO YOU THINK THEY'LL DO TO US, DANIEL?

I DON'T KNOW, SHADRACH. BUT I AM SURE OF THIS, GOD IS WITH US.

SOON AFTER THE PRISONERS REACH THE CITY, DANIEL AND SEVERAL OTHERS ARE BROUGHT BEFORE AN OFFICER OF KING NEBUCHADNEZZAR.

AS NOBLES FROM JERUSALEM, YOU WILL BE GIVEN A CHANCE TO TRY OUT FOR POSITIONS IN THE KING'S COURT. BUT I WARN YOU—ONLY THE SMARTEST AND STRONGEST CAN PASS OUR TESTS.

FOR DAYS THE YOUNG MEN ARE GIVEN EXAMINATIONS TO TEST THEIR PHYSICAL STRENGTH AND MENTAL ALERTNESS.

THIS IS THE LAST TEST. BY TOMORROW YOU WILL KNOW HOW MANY PASSED.

WHAT IF WE FAIL?

WE'VE DONE OUR BEST—THAT'S ALL WE CAN DO.

133

OUR BIBLE IN PICTURES
The Statue
FROM DANIEL 2: 16-48

King Nebuchadnezzar is furious! His wise men cannot tell him what he has dreamed. So he orders all of them put to death--including Daniel and his three friends, Shadrach, Meshach, and Abednego. Daniel asks for permission to speak to the king.

YOU HAVE UNTIL TOMORROW AT THIS HOUR-- BUT NOT ONE MINUTE MORE.

O KING, GIVE ME TIME AND I WILL TELL YOU WHAT YOU DREAMED.

DANIEL RUSHES BACK TO HIS FRIENDS WITH THE GOOD NEWS.

BUT, DANIEL, NO MAN ON EARTH CAN DO WHAT YOU HAVE PROMISED TO DO.

YOU ARE RIGHT-- NO MAN CAN DO IT, BUT GOD CAN. AND WE WILL ASK HIM TO GIVE US THE ANSWER.

135

DANIEL RELAYS THE GOOD NEWS TO HIS HEBREW FRIENDS.

THE KING HAS MADE ME RULER OVER BABYLON AND EACH OF YOU HAS AN IMPORTANT OFFICE IN THE KINGDOM.

THAT'S WONDERFUL!

BUT THE NEWS DOES NOT PLEASE THE KING'S OTHER ADVISERS.

SO THE KING HAS PUT THIS YOUNG HEBREW OVER **US!** WE MUST GET RID OF HIM.

NOT NOW-- HE'S TOO POWERFUL! BUT IF WE CAN TURN THE KING AGAINST DANIEL'S FRIENDS, WE MIGHT BE ABLE TO CAUSE DANIEL TROUBLE.

THEIR OPPORTUNITY COMES WHEN THE KING BUILDS A STATUE AND ORDERS HIS OFFICIALS TO WORSHIP IT--OR BE THROWN INTO A FIERY FURNACE.

THE KING IS PLAYING RIGHT INTO OUR HANDS --HE DOESN'T KNOW THAT HEBREWS WILL WORSHIP ONLY THEIR GOD.

DANIEL HOLDS TOO HIGH A POSITION FOR ANY ONE OF US TO REPORT ON HIM-- BUT NOT HIS FRIENDS...

RIGHT--AND TOMORROW WHEN THE TRUMPET SOUNDS FOR ALL MEN TO BOW BEFORE THE STATUE, WE'LL KEEP OUR EYES ON SHADRACH, MESHACH, AND ABEDNEGO.

OUR BIBLE IN PICTURES
Trial by Fire
FROM DANIEL 3: 1-25

AT KING NEBUCHADNEZZAR'S COMMAND, A GIANT STATUE--90 FEET HIGH--IS BUILT ON THE PLAINS OF DURA. ALL OF THE OFFICIALS OF BABYLON ARE ORDERED TO WORSHIP IT. THE HOUR OF WORSHIP COMES-- THE MOMENT FOR WHICH THE KING'S JEALOUS ADVISERS HAVE BEEN WAITING...

THE MUSICIANS HAVE TAKEN THEIR PLACES. THE SIGNAL WILL SOON BE GIVEN-- THE ONE THAT MEANS DEATH TO DANIEL'S FRIENDS-- SHADRACH, MESHACH, AND ABEDNEGO!

MUSIC FILLS THE AIR-- SOLEMNLY THE OFFICIALS OF BABYLON BOW DOWN AND WORSHIP THE GOLDEN STATUE--ALL BUT SHADRACH, MESHACH, AND ABEDNEGO.

SEE? THEY REFUSE TO BOW DOWN!

138

139

141

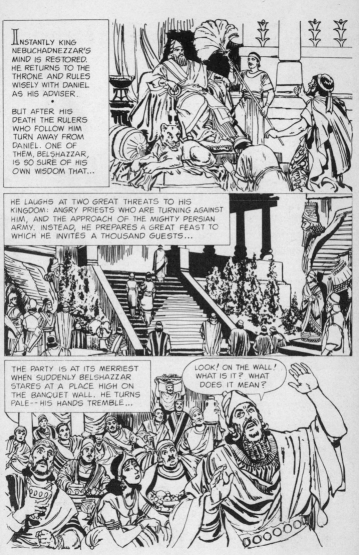

INSTANTLY KING NEBUCHADNEZZAR'S MIND IS RESTORED. HE RETURNS TO THE THRONE AND RULES WISELY WITH DANIEL AS HIS ADVISER.

BUT AFTER HIS DEATH THE RULERS WHO FOLLOW HIM TURN AWAY FROM DANIEL. ONE OF THEM, BELSHAZZAR, IS SO SURE OF HIS OWN WISDOM THAT...

HE LAUGHS AT TWO GREAT THREATS TO HIS KINGDOM: ANGRY PRIESTS WHO ARE TURNING AGAINST HIM, AND THE APPROACH OF THE MIGHTY PERSIAN ARMY. INSTEAD, HE PREPARES A GREAT FEAST TO WHICH HE INVITES A THOUSAND GUESTS...

THE PARTY IS AT ITS MERRIEST WHEN SUDDENLY BELSHAZZAR STARES AT A PLACE HIGH ON THE BANQUET WALL. HE TURNS PALE-- HIS HANDS TREMBLE...

LOOK! ON THE WALL! WHAT IS IT? WHAT DOES IT MEAN?

Handwriting on the Wall

FROM DANIEL 5: 7—6: 14

IT IS MIDNIGHT! OUTSIDE THE WALLS OF BABYLON THE PERSIAN ARMY WAITS FOR TRAITORS WITHIN TO OPEN THE CITY GATES. BUT INSIDE-- IN THE BANQUET HALL OF THE PALACE-- KING BELSHAZZAR EATS AND DRINKS MERRILY WITH HIS GUESTS. SUDDENLY HE SEES A HAND WRITE FOUR WORDS ON THE WALL.

MENE MENE TEKEL UPHARSIN

144

BEFORE MORNING THE CITY IS IN THE HANDS OF THE ENEMY. BELSHAZZAR IS KILLED. DANIEL IS BROUGHT BEFORE DARIUS, THE COMMANDER, WHO RECOGNIZES DANIEL'S ABILITY AS A LEADER.

YOU WILL RULE OVER MY NOBLES AS LONG AS YOU OBEY ME.

DARIUS FINDS DANIEL VERY WISE AND OFTEN TURNS TO HIM FOR ADVICE.

DARIUS HAS APPOINTED DANIEL RULER OVER ALL OF US.

WE MUST GET RID OF HIM-- AND I KNOW JUST HOW TO DO IT!

O KING, YOUR NOBLES, WHO HONOR YOU ABOVE ALL, BEG YOU TO SIGN THIS LAW SO THAT **EVERYONE** WILL HONOR YOU. IT FORBIDS ANYONE TO BOW DOWN TO ANY GOD OR MAN BUT YOU, FOR THIRTY DAYS.

IF YOU WANT SUCH A LAW, I'LL SIGN IT.

146

147

148

MY GOD HAS SHUT THE LIONS' MOUTHS!

THE KING IS OVERJOYED, AND ORDERS A ROPE THROWN DOWN, AND DANIEL IS PULLED OUT OF THE DEN. THEN HE SENDS FOR THE NOBLES WHO PLOTTED DANIEL'S DEATH.

YOU SENT DANIEL TO THE LIONS -- NOW WE'LL SEE HOW **YOU** LIKE IT!

GUARDS! THROW THEM INTO THE DEN!

THEN DARIUS ISSUES A DECREE...

I, DARIUS, COMMAND ALL PEOPLE IN THIS KINGDOM TO HONOR THE GOD THAT DANIEL WORSHIPS AND SERVES.

AND FOR THE REST OF HIS LIFE, DANIEL HELPS TO RULE BABYLON, THE COUNTRY HE ENTERED AS A CAPTIVE. AGAINST ALL ODDS, HE BOLDLY STANDS FOR GOD-- AND GOD REWARDS HIM.

Twelve Men of God

THE LAST TWELVE BOOKS OF THE OLD TESTAMENT ARE CALLED THE MINOR PROPHETS. EACH IS NAMED FOR A MAN WHOM GOD CALLED TO SPEAK FOR HIM AT A CRUCIAL TIME IN THE HISTORY OF ISRAEL AND JUDAH.

HOSEA -- the Prophet of Love

HOSEA LOVES HIS WIFE, GOMER, VERY MUCH. BUT ONE DAY SHE RUNS AWAY. HOSEA IS BROKENHEARTED. THEN SUDDENLY HE SEES THAT THE PEOPLE OF ISRAEL HAVE TREATED GOD THE WAY GOMER HAS TREATED HIM. GOD LOVES HIS PEOPLE, BUT THEY HAVE RUN AWAY TO WORSHIP IDOLS.

CAN GOD FORGIVE THEM? "YES," HOSEA SAYS, "FOR I CAN FORGIVE GOMER, AND GOD'S LOVE IS GREATER THAN MINE."

"GOD LOVES YOU. HE WILL FORGIVE YOUR SINS IF YOU CONFESS THEM AND WORSHIP HIM." THIS IS HOSEA'S MESSAGE TO THE PEOPLE OF ISRAEL.

AMOS -- and the Crooked Wall

JOEL -- and the Plague of Locusts

LIKE A MIGHTY ARMY DESTROYING EVERYTHING IN ITS PATH, MILLIONS OF LOCUSTS SWARM OVER THE LAND OF JUDAH. THEY DEVOUR THE CROPS -- LEAVING ONLY BARREN FIELDS BEHIND.

"WHAT WILL WE DO?" THE PEOPLE CRY.

THE PROPHET JOEL ANSWERS: "REPENT OF YOUR SINS. SEEK GOD'S HELP, AND HE WILL RESTORE THE LAND."

THEN HE ADDS THIS PROMISE: "ONE DAY GOD WILL SEND HIS HOLY SPIRIT INTO THE HEARTS OF HIS PEOPLE." (THIS PROPHECY CAME TRUE WHEN THE HOLY SPIRIT DESCENDED UPON JESUS' DISCIPLES ON THE DAY OF PENTECOST -- ACTS 2.)

AMOS, A SHEPHERD OF JUDAH, IS WATCHING HIS SHEEP WHEN GOD CALLS HIM TO A DANGEROUS JOB. "GO," GOD SAYS, "TO THE NEIGHBORING COUNTRY OF ISRAEL AND TELL THE PEOPLE THAT THEY ARE GOING TO BE PUNISHED FOR THEIR SINS."

WITHOUT PROTESTING, AMOS ACCEPTS THE JOB AND GOES TO THE CITY OF BETHEL IN ISRAEL.

"PREPARE TO MEET THY GOD," HE TELLS THE PEOPLE OF ISRAEL, "FOR YOU ARE LIKE A CROOKED WALL THAT MUST BE DESTROYED BEFORE A NEW ONE CAN BE BUILT."

OBADIAH -- the Angry Prophet

JONAH -- the Man Who Ran Away

OBADIAH IS ANGRY AT JUDAH'S NEIGHBOR, THE NATION OF EDOM. "YOU CHEERED," HE CRIES TO EDOM, "WHEN BABYLON DESTROYED JERUSALEM. YOU HELPED TO ROB THE CITY OF ITS TREASURES. YOU CAPTURED THE PEOPLE AS THEY TRIED TO ESCAPE AND TURNED THEM OVER TO THE ENEMY."

THEN HE PREDICTS EDOM'S PUNISHMENT: "BECAUSE YOUR CAPITAL CITY IS PROTECTED BY ROCKY CLIFFS, YOU THINK IT CANNOT BE DESTROYED. BUT IT CAN! AND IT WILL -- AS WILL EVERY NATION THAT DISOBEYS GOD."

NINEVEH IS ONE OF THE MOST WICKED CITIES IN THE WORLD. SO, WHEN GOD TELLS JONAH TO GO TO NINEVEH WITH A MESSAGE TO SAVE THE CITY FROM ITS ENEMIES, JONAH RUNS THE OTHER WAY.

BUT AFTER A LESSON FROM GOD, JONAH OBEYS. HE TELLS NINEVEH TO REPENT OF ITS SINS -- AND HE PREACHES HIS MESSAGE SO SUCCESSFULLY THAT THE CITY DOES REPENT AND IS SAVED FROM DESTRUCTION.

THE MESSAGE OF THE BOOK OF JONAH IS THIS: GOD LOVES ALL PEOPLE. THOSE WHO KNOW GOD MUST TELL OTHERS ABOUT HIM.

MICAH -- Champion of the Poor

NAHUM Condemns a City

MICAH, A SMALL-TOWN PROPHET, IS A CHAMPION OF THE POOR. HE DARES TO CONDEMN THE WEALTHY LEADERS OF JUDAH AND ISRAEL.

"YOU HATE JUSTICE," HE SHOUTS, "AND YOU OPPRESS THE POOR. BECAUSE YOU DO, JUDAH AND ISRAEL HAVE BECOME SO WEAK AND CORRUPT THAT THEY WILL BE DESTROYED."

WHEN THE PEOPLE ASK WHAT GOD EXPECTS THEM TO DO, MICAH ANSWERS: "DO JUSTLY, LOVE MERCY, AND WALK HUMBLY WITH THY GOD."

AND TO THOSE WHO WILL LISTEN HE MAKES A WONDERFUL PROMISE: "IN THE LITTLE TOWN OF BETHLEHEM A SAVIOR WILL BE BORN -- A SAVIOR WHOSE KINGDOM OF PEACE WILL LAST FOREVER."

WHEN THE PROPHET JONAH WARNED NINEVEH OF ITS WICKEDNESS, THE CITY REPENTED -- AND WAS SPARED.

NOW, ONE HUNDRED AND FIFTY YEARS LATER, ANOTHER PROPHET, NAHUM, IS CALLED TO CONDEMN NINEVEH FOR RETURNING TO A LIFE OF SIN.

"THE LORD IS SLOW TO ANGER," NAHUM TELLS THE CITY, "BUT HE IS NOT BLIND. HE WILL NOT LET THE WICKED GO UNPUNISHED."

THIS TIME THE CITY IS NOT SPARED -- THE ARMIES OF BABYLON SO COMPLETELY DESTROY NINEVEH THAT IT IS NEVER REBUILT.

HABAKKUK -- The Man Who Asks Questions

HABAKKUK IS A MAN WHO ASKS QUESTIONS -- OF GOD.

HABAKKUK: THE PEOPLE OF JUDAH ARE GETTING MORE WICKED EVERY DAY. HOW LONG WILL THEY GO UNPUNISHED?

GOD: NOT FOR LONG. THE BABYLONIANS ARE COMING. I AM USING THEM TO TEACH JUDAH THAT EVIL MUST BE DESTROYED.

HABAKKUK: THE BABYLONIANS? AREN'T THEY MORE WICKED THAN JUDAH?

GOD: YES, BUT HAVE FAITH. IN TIME YOU WILL UNDERSTAND MY PLANS.

IN THE MIDST OF ALL THE EVIL AROUND HIM, HABAKKUK IS COMFORTED IN KNOWING THAT GOD IS IN CHARGE OF THE WORLD. "GOD IS IN HIS HOLY TEMPLE," HABAKKUK SAYS, "AND NO MATTER WHAT HAPPENS, I AM NOT AFRAID, FOR THE LORD IS MY STRENGTH."

ZECHARIAH and the Triumphal Entry

ZECHARIAH IS A FRIEND OF HAGGAI AND WORKS WITH HIM TO REBUILD THE TEMPLE IN JERUSALEM. BUT ZECHARIAH SEES BEYOND THE STONE AND WOOD OF THE BUILDING -- HE SEES THE GLORIOUS COMING OF CHRIST: "BEHOLD," HE SAYS, "THY KING COMETH RIDING UNTO THEE."

(THIS PROPHECY CAME TRUE WHEN CHRIST RODE INTO JERUSALEM ON THE DAY WE REMEMBER AS PALM SUNDAY.)

ZEPHANIAH: Repent or Die

"THE DAY OF THE LORD IS AT HAND," ZEPHANIAH WARNED JUDAH. "GOD WILL PUNISH ALL NATIONS OF THE EARTH THAT HAVE DISOBEYED HIM. NEITHER GOLD NOR SILVER WILL BE ABLE TO DELIVER THOSE WHO HAVE TURNED FROM GOD."

ZEPHANIAH PLEADS WITH HIS PEOPLE TO REPENT AND SEEK GOD'S FORGIVENESS. "THOSE WHO DO," HE PROMISES, "WILL LIVE IN PEACE UNDER THE RULE OF GOD."

HAGGAI -- A Temple Builder

WHEN THE HEBREWS FIRST RETURN TO JERUSALEM -- AFTER YEARS OF CAPTIVITY IN BABYLON -- THEIR FIRST THOUGHT IS TO REBUILD THE TEMPLE. THEY START -- BUT THEY SOON GET DISCOURAGED AND QUIT. FOR FIFTEEN YEARS NOTHING IS DONE.

GOD SPEAKS TO HAGGAI AND HE TAKES THE MESSAGE TO THE PEOPLE.

"BUILD GOD'S TEMPLE," HE PREACHES. AND IN FOUR YEARS IT IS BUILT!

MALACHI -- The Final Warning

THE PEOPLE OF JUDAH HAVE RETURNED TO JERUSALEM FROM CAPTIVITY IN BABYLON -- THE TEMPLE HAS BEEN REBUILT. BUT STILL THEY ARE UNHAPPY. AND MALACHI TELLS THEM WHY --

"YOU DO NOT SHOW RESPECT TO GOD. YOU WOULD NOT DARE BRING CHEAP GIFTS TO THE GOVERNOR. YET YOU BRING CHEAP AND FAULTY OFFERINGS TO GOD."

"GOD KNOWS THOSE WHO ARE FAITHFUL TO HIM. HE WILL REWARD THEM. BUT THE UNFAITHFUL WILL PERISH AS STUBBLE IN THE BURNING FIELDS AFTER THE HARVEST."

The Unfaithful Wife

FROM HOSEA 1—13

THE NORTHERN KINGDOM OF ISRAEL HAS BECOME A RICH AND POWERFUL NATION. BUT UNDER THE LEADERSHIP OF THEIR PRIESTS AND NOBLES, THE PEOPLE TURN FROM GOD TO WORSHIP IDOLS. THE COUNTRY BECOMES SO CORRUPT THAT GOD SENDS THE PROPHET HOSEA WITH A MESSAGE TO SAVE ISRAEL-- IF ISRAEL WILL LISTEN...

ONE DAY HOSEA RETURNS HOME TO FIND THE CHILDREN ALONE AND CRYING...

WHAT IS THE MATTER? WHERE IS YOUR MOTHER?

SHE LEFT WITH SOME OTHER MAN. SHE WAS LAUGHING AND HAVING A GOOD TIME. O FATHER, I THINK SHE LOVES HIM MORE THAN SHE DOES US.

HOSEA CAN HARDLY BELIEVE THAT HIS WIFE, GOMER, WOULD LEAVE HIM AND THE CHILDREN. HE SETS OUT TO LOOK FOR HER.

HAVE YOU SEEN MY WIFE?

NO--BUT PEOPLE SAY SHE WENT TO ANOTHER CITY.

154

155

Dangerous Mission

FROM AMOS 1—9

THE ISRAELITES WERE TURNING THEIR BACKS ON GOD AND HIS TEACHINGS TO WORSHIP IDOLS. BUT GOD LOVED HIS PEOPLE AND SENT TWO PROPHETS WITH MESSAGES THAT WOULD HELP THEM -- IF THEY WOULD LISTEN. ONE WAS HOSEA, WHO TOLD THEM OF GOD'S FORGIVING LOVE; THE OTHER WAS AMOS, WHOSE MESSAGE IS FOUND IN THE BOOK THAT BEARS HIS NAME.

WHAT BRINGS YOU HERE, STRANGER?

GOD SENT ME TO WARN ISRAEL. THE PEOPLE MUST TURN FROM EVIL -- BEFORE IT IS TOO LATE.

AMOS IS TENDING HIS SHEEP ON THE HILLS OF JUDAH WHEN GOD CALLS HIM. "TAKE MY MESSAGE TO THE KINGDOM OF ISRAEL," GOD SAYS. AMOS SETS OUT AT ONCE, CROSSES THE BORDER INTO ISRAEL, AND GOES STRAIGHT TO BETHEL, THE COUNTRY'S MAIN PLACE OF WORSHIP.

YOU'RE ON A DANGEROUS MISSION. THE KING, PRINCES, AND PRIESTS ARE THE WORST SINNERS OF ALL.

THEN MY MESSAGE IS FOR THEM. FOR GOD HAS SENT ME TO WARN EVILDOERS THAT THEY WILL BE PUNISHED.

157

IF THOSE COUNTRIES DESERVE PUNISHMENT, HOW MUCH MORE DO **YOU**, O ISRAEL! GOD HAS LOVED AND PROTECTED YOU. BUT YOU HAVE SINNED AGAINST HIM. YOU CHEAT THE POOR; YOU WORSHIP IDOLS. FOR THIS YOU WILL BE PUNISHED. YOUR ENEMIES WILL DEFEAT YOU AND TAKE YOU AS CAPTIVES-- SO, PREPARE TO MEET THY GOD!

GO BACK TO THE HILLS AND PREACH TO YOUR OWN PEOPLE.

GOD SENT ME TO PREACH TO **YOU**! AND FOR **YOUR** SINS, O HIGH PRIEST, YOU WILL BE AMONG THOSE WHO DIE IN CAPTIVITY.

STOP THAT KIND OF TALK OR YOU'LL BE PUT TO DEATH!

THE HIGH PRIEST ACCUSES AMOS OF TREASON -- BUT EVEN THIS DOES NOT STOP AMOS FROM DELIVERING GOD'S MESSAGE TO ISRAEL. BUT ISRAEL DOES NOT REPENT...

THE BIBLE DOES NOT SAY WHAT HAPPENS TO AMOS. IT ONLY RECORDS HIS MESSAGE--WHICH COMES TRUE IN LESS THAN FORTY YEARS. THE ASSYRIANS CONQUER ISRAEL AND TAKE ITS PEOPLE AWAY AS CAPTIVES. THEY NEVER RETURN!

The Runaway

FROM JONAH 1: 1-12

GOD CALLED THE PROPHET JONAH FOR A SPECIAL FOREIGN ASSIGNMENT. THE WAY JONAH CARRIES IT OUT IS FOUND IN THE BOOK THAT BEARS HIS NAME.

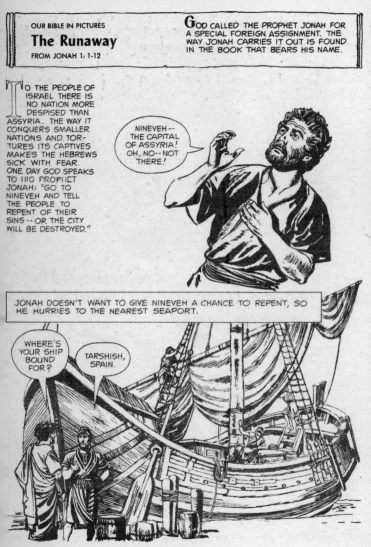

TO THE PEOPLE OF ISRAEL THERE IS NO NATION MORE DESPISED THAN ASSYRIA. THE WAY IT CONQUERS SMALLER NATIONS AND TORTURES ITS CAPTIVES MAKES THE HEBREWS SICK WITH FEAR. ONE DAY GOD SPEAKS TO HIS PROPHET JONAH: "GO TO NINEVEH AND TELL THE PEOPLE TO REPENT OF THEIR SINS -- OR THE CITY WILL BE DESTROYED."

NINEVEH -- THE CAPITAL OF ASSYRIA! OH, NO-- NOT THERE!

JONAH DOESN'T WANT TO GIVE NINEVEH A CHANCE TO REPENT, SO HE HURRIES TO THE NEAREST SEAPORT.

WHERE'S YOUR SHIP BOUND FOR?

TARSHISH, SPAIN.

160

BUT JONAH IS ASHAMED TO PRAY TO GOD. INSTEAD, HE HURRIES UP ON DECK...

SOMEONE ON THIS SHIP HAS DONE EVIL AND BROUGHT THIS STORM UPON US.

LET'S DRAW LOTS* TO SEE WHO IT IS.

* THE CASTING OF LOTS WAS A CUSTOM USED BY ANCIENT PEOPLES TO DECIDE IMPORTANT ISSUES. THEY BELIEVED A DIVINE POWER WOULD CAUSE THE RIGHT LOT TO BE DRAWN.

QUICKLY THE NAMES OF ALL ON BOARD ARE WRITTEN ON BITS OF POTTERY AND PLACED IN THE FOLD OF A SAILOR'S GARMENT.

DRAW ONE. THEN WE'LL KNOW WHO THE GUILTY MAN IS.

JONAH! WHAT HAVE YOU DONE TO BRING THIS STORM ON US?

I AM A HEBREW -- AND I HAVE RUN AWAY FROM GOD.

WHAT MUST WE DO TO SAVE OUR LIVES?

THROW ME INTO THE SEA!

161

OUR BIBLE IN PICTURES

The Second Call

FROM JONAH 1: 13—3: 3

FOR THREE DAYS AND THREE NIGHTS JONAH IS IN THE BODY OF THE FISH. THEN GOD CAUSES THE FISH TO CAST JONAH UP ON THE BEACH. AND ONCE AGAIN GOD SPEAKS TO JONAH: "GO TO NINEVEH AND TELL THE PEOPLE THEY MUST REPENT OF THEIR SINS -- OR THE CITY WILL BE DESTROYED."

A Wicked City–an Angry Prophet–and God

FROM JONAH 3: 4—4: 11

AT SUNRISE THE GATES OF MIGHTY NINEVEH SWING OPEN. TRADERS, WAITING OUTSIDE, ENTER THE CITY. MERCHANTS OPEN THEIR SHOPS. SLAVE TRADERS DRIVE CAPTIVES TO THE AUCTION BLOCK TO BE SOLD TO THE HIGHEST BIDDER. SUDDENLY JONAH, GOD'S PROPHET, APPEARS IN THE STREETS.

IN FORTY DAYS, NINEVEH SHALL BE DESTROYED FOR ITS WICKEDNESS.

164

DID YOU HEAR WHAT HE SAID? NINEVEH WILL BE DESTROYED!

IN FORTY DAYS -- WHAT CAN WE DO?

NEWS OF JONAH'S WARNING TRAVELS FAST; WHEN IT REACHES THE KING, HE ISSUES AN ORDER.

PRAY TO GOD FOR MERCY. IF WE REPENT OF OUR SINS, PERHAPS GOD WILL FORGIVE US.

EVERYWHERE THROUGHOUT THE GREAT CITY, PEOPLE FALL ON THEIR KNEES IN PRAYER.

I SHOULD NOT HAVE WARNED THESE ENEMIES OF MY PEOPLE. GOD IS MERCIFUL AND HE MAY FORGIVE THEM.

AFTER DELIVERING HIS MESSAGE, JONAH GOES OUTSIDE THE CITY TO WAIT AND SEE WHAT WILL HAPPEN TO NINEVEH. GOD CAUSES A LARGE VINE TO GROW UP AND SHELTER JONAH.

I'D DIE FROM THE HEAT OF THE SUN IF IT WEREN'T FOR THE SHADE OF THIS VINE.

BUT--SUDDENLY--THE VINE DIES AND THE HOT SUN BEATS DOWN ON JONAH.

I'D RATHER BE DEAD THAN SUFFER LIKE THIS!

LORD, WHY DIDN'T YOU SPARE THE VINE?

GOD ANSWERS: WOULD YOU HAVE ME SPARE A VINE, JONAH, BUT NOT SPARE NINEVEH WITH ITS 120,000 INNOCENT CHILDREN?

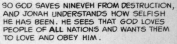

SO GOD SAVES NINEVEH FROM DESTRUCTION, AND JONAH UNDERSTANDS HOW SELFISH HE HAS BEEN. HE SEES THAT GOD LOVES PEOPLE OF **ALL** NATIONS AND WANTS THEM TO LOVE AND OBEY HIM.

The Final Message

FROM THE BOOK OF MALACHI

THE VOICE OF THE PROPHET MALACHI IS THE LAST TO
BE HEARD IN THE STORY OF THE OLD TESTAMENT. BUT
BEFORE WE HEAR HIS FINAL MESSAGE--WHICH IS
FOUND IN THE BOOK THAT BEARS HIS NAME --
LET US BRIEFLY REVIEW THE HISTORY OF THE
PEOPLE TO WHOM HE SPOKE.

IN OUR STORY OF THE BIBLE WE
HAVE BEEN TRACING THE LIVES OF
THE PEOPLE WHO DESCENDED FROM
ABRAHAM. GOD CALLED HIM TO BE
THE FATHER OF A NATION THAT WOULD
TEACH THE WORLD ABOUT THE ONE
TRUE GOD. ABRAHAM OBEYED GOD AND
WENT TO CANAAN WHERE HIS FAMILY
LIVED AND GREW. HIS GRANDSON, JACOB
(OR ISRAEL), BECAME THE FATHER OF
12 SONS. THEIR FAMILIES WERE CALLED
THE 12 TRIBES OF ISRAEL.

WHEN A FAMINE STRUCK CANAAN THE TRIBES WENT DOWN TO EGYPT WHERE THEY LIVED FOR MANY YEARS. BUT AFTER A TIME THE EGYPTIANS TURNED AGAINST THE ISRAELITES AND FORCED THEM TO WORK AS SLAVES. THE PEOPLE CRIED TO GOD FOR HELP...

GOD HEARD THE CRIES OF HIS PEOPLE AND SENT MOSES TO LEAD THEM OUT OF EGYPT -- ACROSS THE RED SEA -- AND BACK TO THE PROMISED LAND OF CANAAN. WITH GOD'S HELP THEY CONQUERED THE LAND AND MADE IT THEIR HOME. FOR MANY YEARS JUDGES RULED OVER THE TRIBES OF ISRAEL, BUT THE PEOPLE LONGED FOR A KING.

GOD HEARD THEIR PLEA AND GAVE THEM A KING, SAUL. HE WAS FOLLOWED BY DAVID, WHO BUILT ISRAEL INTO A POWERFUL NATION. BUT IN THE YEARS THAT FOLLOWED, THE PEOPLE TURNED FROM GOD TO WORSHIP IDOLS. THEY QUARRELED AMONG THEMSELVES, AND THE NATION WAS SPLIT INTO TWO KINGDOMS -- ISRAEL IN THE NORTH AND JUDAH IN THE SOUTH. WEAK AND CORRUPT, THEY WERE OPEN TO THE ATTACKS OF STRONGER NATIONS AROUND THEM.

IN TIME BOTH KINGDOMS WERE CONQUERED. MANY OF THE PEOPLE WERE TAKEN AWAY TO FOREIGN LANDS. AFTER 70 YEARS OF CAPTIVITY, THE JEWS WERE ALLOWED TO RETURN TO JUDAH AND REBUILD JERUSALEM.

BUT STILL THE PEOPLE WERE UNHAPPY, AND THE PROPHET MALACHI TELLS THEM WHY...

DO YOU CALL THAT GOD'S SHARE OF YOUR GRAIN? HOW CAN YOU BE HAPPY WHEN YOU ROB GOD? BRING YOUR RIGHTFUL GIFTS AND OFFERINGS TO GOD, AND YOU WILL PROSPER.

BUT PEOPLE WHO CHEAT AND BRING NONE OF THEIR GRAIN TO THE TEMPLE PROSPER MORE THAN WE DO.

GOD KNOWS WHO LOVES AND OBEYS HIM. HE WILL REWARD THE RIGHTEOUS AND PUNISH THE WICKED.

WHEN WILL HE DO THIS?

FIRST, GOD WILL SEND A PROPHET AS HIS MESSENGER TO GET THE PEOPLE READY. THEN THE LORD HIMSELF WILL COME AND DELIVER HIS OWN PEOPLE FROM EVIL. BUT HE WILL DESTROY THE WICKED WHO DISOBEY.

SO, WITH A WARNING -- AND A PROMISE -- THE OLD TESTAMENT ENDS. BUT TO THE JEWS THE QUESTION REMAINS: WHEN WILL THE GREAT DELIVERER COME?

The Years of Waiting

THE LAND OF JUDAH IS STILL UNDER THE RULE OF THE
PERSIANS WHEN ALEXANDER, THE YOUNG KING OF MACEDONIA,
SETS OUT TO CONQUER THE WORLD.
RIDING HIS FAMOUS HORSE, BUCEPHALUS,
HE LEADS HIS ARMY AGAINST THE COUNTRIES
OF THE MIGHTY PERSIAN EMPIRE. ONE
AFTER ANOTHER THEY FALL, AND IN 332 B.C....

THE CITY WAITS IN TERROR! BUT WHEN ALEXANDER'S ARMY COMES IN SIGHT, THE HIGH PRIEST OPENS THE GATES AND LEADS A PROCESSION OUT TO GREET THE CONQUEROR. ALEXANDER RECOGNIZES THE PRIEST AS A MAN OF GOD AND BOWS BEFORE HIM. THEN HE ENTERS THE CITY AND WORSHIPS IN THE TEMPLE. UNDER THE RULE OF THIS DARING YOUNG WARRIOR THE JEWS ARE ALLOWED TO KEEP THEIR OWN RELIGIOUS CUSTOMS -- AND THEY ARE HAPPY.

BUT -- SUDDENLY -- ALEXANDER DIES... AND THE GIANT EMPIRE IS DIVIDED AMONG HIS GENERALS. WHEN THE RULER OVER JUDAH COMMANDS THE PEOPLE TO WORSHIP AN IDOL, A PRIEST SLAYS THE KING'S MESSENGER. THIS BOLD ACT STIRS ALL JUDAH TO REVOLT...

UNDER THE LEADERSHIP OF THE PRIEST'S BRAVE FAMILY (KNOWN AS THE MACCABEES), THE JEWS DRIVE THE ENEMY FROM THEIR LAND. ONE OF THE FIRST THINGS THEY DO IS TO REDEDICATE THE TEMPLE, WHICH THE ENEMY HAD USED TO WORSHIP IDOLS. FOR A HUNDRED GLORIOUS YEARS JUDAH IS FREE!

BUT ONCE AGAIN A CONQUEROR COMES FROM ACROSS THE MEDITERRANEAN SEA. ROMAN SHIPS AND ROMAN SOLDIERS CONQUER EVERYTHING IN THEIR PATH. AND IN 63 B.C. THE MIGHTY ROMAN ARMY TAKES JERUSALEM. AGAIN JUDAH IS DOWN-- AND THIS TIME IT IS TOO WEAK TO RISE.

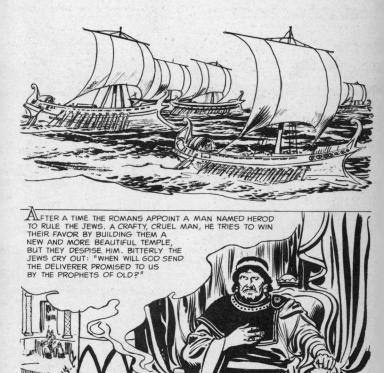

AFTER A TIME THE ROMANS APPOINT A MAN NAMED HEROD TO RULE THE JEWS. A CRAFTY, CRUEL MAN, HE TRIES TO WIN THEIR FAVOR BY BUILDING THEM A NEW AND MORE BEAUTIFUL TEMPLE, BUT THEY DESPISE HIM. BITTERLY THE JEWS CRY OUT: "WHEN WILL GOD SEND THE DELIVERER PROMISED TO US BY THE PROPHETS OF OLD?"

IN BIBLE TIMES

THE Bible

IS THE MOST INTERESTING BOOK EVER WRITTEN. BUT HOW MUCH DO **YOU** KNOW ABOUT IT? FOR EXAMPLE—SEE IF YOU CAN MATCH THESE WORDS TO THEIR BIBLE-TIMES PICTURES. CORRECT ANSWERS ARE AT THE BOTTOM OF THE PAGE.

1. AN AQUEDUCT WAS...

A. A WATER BIRD LIKE A DUCK.

B. A SHIP WITH A PROW LIKE A DUCK.

C. A STRUCTURE THAT CARRIED WATER.

2. A PERSIAN WAS...

A. AN ORIENTAL CAT.

B. SOMEONE WHO LIVED IN PERSIA.

C. SOMEONE WHO TALKED PERSIAN TO PERSIAN ON AN ANCIENT TELEPHONE.

3. A HOMER WAS...

A. A FORM OF HOMING PIGEON.

B. A CIRCUIT CLOUT IN AN ANCIENT BALL GAME!

C. A UNIT OF MEASURE EQUAL TO ABOUT 11⅔ BUSHELS.

ANSWERS 1-c; 2-b; 3-c

173

The Bible

THE BIBLE AND ARCHAEOLOGY

THIS ANCIENT BABYLONIAN SEAL FROM ABOUT 3000 B.C. LOOKS LIKE THE BIBLE STORY OF EVE REACHING FOR THE FORBIDDEN FRUIT.

"...AND THERE WAS FAMINE IN THE LAND" (GEN. 12:10). AN OLD EGYPTIAN DRAWING SHOWS A THIN, STARVING MAN LEADING HIS OXEN.

"HEZEKIAH...MADE A POOL, AND A CONDUIT, AND BROUGHT WATER INTO THE CITY."

THIS 1777 FT. LONG TUNNEL WAS BUILT IN 701 B.C. IT WAS RE-DISCOVERED IN 1838. IT STILL CARRIES WATER FROM THE GIHON SPRING TO THE POOL OF SILOAM.

THE MOABITE STONE, CARVED ABOUT 850 B.C., CONFIRMS THE BIBLE RECORD FOUND IN II KINGS 3:5 OF THE MOABITE KING WHO REBELLED AGAINST ISRAEL.

IN 1947 AN ARAB BOY FOUND A CAVE THAT HELD SEVERAL ANCIENT POTS FILLED WITH SCROLLS. EXAMINATION BY ARCHAEOLOGISTS PROVED THE SCROLLS INCLUDED COPIES OF THE BOOK OF ISAIAH WRITTEN ABOUT 100 YEARS BEFORE CHRIST. THEY WERE THE NOW FAMOUS "DEAD SEA SCROLLS".